## ADVANCE PRAISE

"Parenting anxious kids can be hard. As a mom of an anxious child and a very satisfied client of Tonya Crombie's coaching, I highly recommend this book and her work to any parent looking for guidance, assistance, and support to help them on their parenting journey. Her support to me as a parent has allowed me to become the parent my daughter needs."

-**Danielle Droitsch**, mom and certified life coach, Coaching with Danielle, Arlington VA

"As both a parent of an anxious child and a psychologist, Tonya Collings-Crombie's, *Stop Worrying About Your Anxious Child*, offers a fresh perspective and sound, ready-to-use strategies for parents. Through the lens of her personal journey to better understand and support her own anxious (and amazing!) child, Dr. Collings-Crombie shows how to find your inner calm, trust your intuition, and to treat yourself with kindness and compassion. As both a child psychologist, and a parent myself, this book will be an invaluable resource that I can share with families, so I will need to have one to keep and one to share!"

-**LuAnn Keough, Ph.D.** Licensed Psychologist
Licensed School Psychologist Wellesley MA

"Anxiety is on the rise in American children as well as with the parents that are watching their kids in this struggle. In her book, Dr. Crombie presents insightful, practical help that will make parents feel more grounded and have a better understanding of how they place "meaning" into their children's behavior and lives. She communicates in a way to make you feel like you are talking and sharing and learning from a good friend. I will recommend this book to parents in my practice who continue to struggle with their child's anxiety."

-**Paul M. Friedberg, Ph.D.** Licensed Psychologist in the great state of Louisiana who has been working with children and their parents for the past 25 years.

"As a Psychologist, I have come to realize that if I managed to give my children the perfect upbringing, they would suffer for it! Over-protectiveness and worry about our children's well-being is normal, as is clearly stated in this book. Yet reading Dr. Crombie's book strengthens my belief that resiliency and hardiness in our kids comes through tough experiences, both for them, and for us! How we think about those experiences influences our own anxiety, and thus models our coping behaviors (or lack thereof) for our kids.

Dr. Crombie cleverly imparts important psychological and therapeutic principles through a very relaxed, personal, and conversational narrative. In fact, in a different voice, this could very well be mistaken for a textbook on cognitive psychology practices! Many of her principles and techniques are the ones I use with anxious clients in a clinical setting, and yet she delivers her message as if she just stopped by for coffee! Now I have a perfect, easy-to-read book I can offer to parents struggling with these issues to supplement the therapy."

-**John C. Parkhurst, Ph.D.** Psychologist and CEO, Parkhurst Associates Mental Health Services, Washington, DC.

Stop Worrying About Your Anxious Child

# STOP
# *Worrying*
## ABOUT YOUR
# Anxious
# CHILD

*How to Manage Your
Child's Anxiety so
You Can Finally Relax*

Tonya C. Crombie, PhD

NEW YORK

LONDON • NASHVILLE • MELBOURNE • VANCOUVER

# Stop Worrying About Your Anxious Child

## How to Manage Your Child's Anxiety so You Can Finally Relax

Published in New York, New York, by Morgan James Publishing in partnership with Difference Press. Morgan James is a trademark of Morgan James, LLC. www.MorganJamesPublishing.com

ISBN 9781631951015 paperback
ISBN 9781631951022 eBook
ISBN 9781631951039 audio
Library of Congress Control Number: 2020934458

**Cover Design Concept:** Nakita Duncan

**Cover & Interior Design:** Chris Treccani www.3dogcreative.net

**Editor:** Nkechi Obi

**Book Coaching:** The Author Incubator

Morgan James is a proud partner of Habitat for Humanity Peninsula and Greater Williamsburg. Partners in building since 2006.

Get involved today! Visit
MorganJamesPublishing.com/giving-back

*To Bill, for being my biggest cheerleader, my rock, and mostly for always making me laugh.*

# TABLE OF CONTENTS

*Foreword*                                                        *xiii*

Chapter 1:     I Feel You                                          1

Chapter 2:     I've Been There Too, Sister!                        5

Chapter 3:     Here's Where We're Going and
               Where We're Going to End Up                         13

Chapter 4:     It's All Normal—We Just
               Don't Think It Is                                   17

Chapter 5:     Deal with the Haters:
               Handling Judgment                                   33

Chapter 6:     Opinions Are Like A*******:
               What to Do with All of the Advice?                  53

Chapter 7:     Find Your Calm in the Chaos:
               Unfortunately, It's Got to Start
               with You                                            69

Chapter 8:     Coping Strategies—The Good,
               The Bad, and The Ugly                               81

Chapter 9:     Who's in the Circle? Create a Support
               System that Really Supports                         101

Chapter 10:   Putting It All Together          113
Chapter 11:   The Top Three Ways
              I Screwed Up                      121
Chapter 12:   You Got This—Seriously,
              You Do!                           131

*Acknowledgments*                              *137*
*Thank You*                                    *141*
*About the Author*                             *143*

# FOREWORD

I have known Dr. Tonya Crombie for over 10 years, during which time we have shared observations on parenting (our own and others') and life (our own and others'). Being friends with her, I have benefitted from her advice and knowledge countless times, which has always been just a text or a call away. With the publication of "Stop Worrying About Your Anxious Child," I am happy that others will get to share in her wisdom.

As a pediatrician, I daily encounter parents who are struggling to manage their own reactions to their child's unique personality. There are some parts of a child's being that are easy to respond to: when they are calm, for example, or when they are compliant. But when our children are feeling and acting imbalanced or anxious, it is hard to know how to "right the ship" so we can get out of the vortex of anxiety and move forward together in a peaceful way.

In the writing of this book, Tonya has compiled the research and progress she has amassed and put into practice so that other parents will benefit from what she has learned along the way. Reading this book does make you feel that Tonya is your friend, too, and that as you find your way, she will be right beside you with an encouraging word and a couple of recipes to go with it. It makes you feel like you have a friend who knows what it's like and wants you to succeed, but will also laugh with you when it goes terribly awry and you fall flat on your parental face.

Tonya offers strategies for dealing with your own emotions and reactions as you ride the crazy roller coaster of parenting. And when the anxious wing of your child's emotional makeup is winning in his or her body, this book gives you parenting tips to help you calm down and break the cycle so that the "anxiety train," as she calls it, doesn't steamroll your entire family.

Through the tips she has set out, Tonya encourages and teaches you to recognize your own thoughts and feelings and get out of what I like to think of a hamster wheel of "what ifs." Once you are out, you can calm down when others around you are melting down. Once you are calm, she teaches you to recognize your own gut feelings and intuition and to surround yourself with the right people—people who will be honest with you and support you.

When you inevitably mess up, and you will mess up, Tonya encourages you to take a breath, appreciate the progress you have made, and do better next time. Beating yourself up does not move you or your child in a positive direction. With practice, following the steps Tonya has laid out will change your mental dialogue so that you and your child are on the journey together, and not on opposing teams. Learning and then modeling these coping strategies and calming techniques for yourself makes it likely that your child will absorb and incorporate the strategies into his or her own emotional bank.

You may never have had someone simply instruct you to breathe. You may never have tried having a mantra, or practicing biofeedback or meditation. And you probably do not have a "God box." But if you have picked up this book, it means you have wondered how in the world you're going to survive your own worry about your anxious child. I believe that by the time you put the book down, you will have made at least some progress toward calm and peace.

For years I have benefitted from Tonya's advice, and now here it is in writing for all of us to use. Hopefully her strategies will give you confidence to model positive ways to deal with your own worries so that your child can learn to deal with his or hers as well. I am happy to share my friend, Tonya's, advice and wisdom. As she so powerfully puts it, we are all "on a journey to becoming the best mom we can be at a given time." Now that is a journey to which we can all support each other and raise a glass.

-Julie Miley Schlegel, M.D.

CHAPTER 1:

# I Feel You

Having a child who struggles with anxiety sucks!

It's the worst!

If you are reading this right now, you know what I mean. You've experienced it all. You know the fear that grips your stomach each time you start to sense anxiety and panic taking over your sweet baby. You know the pain and heartache when your child is excluded because their anxiety makes them seem different or odd. You've felt the burning anger or shame when another parent judges you for "letting" your child act that way. And you know the feeling of being completely alone like you are the only one in the entire world, or at least in your friend group, who is going through this. But if you only read one sentence in this entire book, I hope you read this one because it's very important: *you are not alone.*

Not even close. While you and I tend to get our ideas about what's going on with everyone else from superficial conversations and by scrolling through our Facebook feed, it just takes a quick Google search to see that anxiety is one of the most common and fastest-growing ailments among many people and especially among our kids.

Anxiety is very, *very* common. But of course, you aren't a statistic. You are a very real parent with a very real child and a very real problem. And even if the statistics say it's common, it feels like you are the only one who is dealing with the nail-biting, the extreme shyness, the unwillingness to try new things, the fidgeting, the inability to sit still, the crying, the tantrums, the defiance, and the "I'm *not* going!" declarations.

Teacher conferences can feel like torture. Playdates can be a nightmare. Birthday parties can go from fun to miserable in 0.2 seconds. You second guess yourself, wonder if you could have done something differently. You feel guilty about things you wish you had tried or wish you hadn't tried. You worry about your child's future. You hate having to deal with those judgey parents but wonder if you should listen to all of the advice they offer. The constant worrying and second-guessing creates conflict between you and your spouse or co-parent or just anyone else who loves your child and has an opinion about what's best.

I hear you. I feel you. I know how you feel because I've been there too. I hope you'll keep reading because I want to share some things I learned on my own turbulent journey of parenting my own beautifully perfect anxious child.

I'd love it if you could imagine that you and I are sitting down and having coffee together. We're going to chat about what it's like because we both know. And because we both know, I'm going to share the things that I've found and have helped me feel better. It just so happens that they are also things I've used to help other parents just like you manage their child's anxiety so that they can relax, enjoy parenthood, and begin to trust in their child's bright future again.

If your dream come true is that your child will learn to cope with their anxiety and have a happy successful life filled with friends, that's my dream too. Let's talk.

If you are ready to feel calmer, if you want your life to feel less chaotic and less stressful-not only for your anxious child but also for you and for your entire family, go grab that cup of coffee, and let's chat.

# CHAPTER 2:

# I've Been There Too, Sister!

Well, if we are going to have coffee, we should probably start by getting to know each other, right? I mean, we already know a little about each other. We're both parents to kids who struggle with anxiety. But of course, there's quite a bit more to both of our stories than just that. Here's just a little bit more of mine.

I've done some really cool things in my life, and I'd love to tell you all about them, but we aren't getting any younger here, and I think you probably want to hear about my struggles with parenting that are so much like yours. And new friend, my struggles were so much like yours, and they still are.

## The Joy of Motherhood

In the beginning, becoming a mother was a dream come true for me. I was that kid who played with dolls for way longer than what was considered cool. So, getting a real-live doll was pretty awesome, and it was only made better by getting a second beautiful live baby doll sixteen short months after the first. I learned how to be a mom from my Irish twins who couldn't have been more different if they tried. There are millions of clichés out there like "motherhood: the toughest job you'll ever love," and in my case, that was totally true (and friend, you are soon going to see that there's nothing I love more than a good cliché. I do. No apologies, either). Everyone always says motherhood is tough but worth it, and until I was a mother, I really had no idea what that meant.

One reason that I love being a mother so much is that it forced me to become a better person. I had to learn and grow and change so much in order to be the best mom I could be. But before you take even one more sip of that coffee or tea or whatever you might be drinking, let me assure you that the best mom I could be was and still is always very far from perfect. I've made mistakes as a mom—some small ones and some biggies. I have regrets. I know there are all sorts of clichés about regret too like "each mistake got you where you are today." And while the wisest part of me actually knows that is true, the simple, less thoughtful, and spiritual part of me regrets a lot of things I said, did, and chose to do as a mom.

Luckily for me, it seems God makes children pretty resilient. As I type these words, my sixteen-year-old is working at a job he hates, but he continues to go to it because he made a commitment, and he knows he has to honor it until he can find something better. And my other child is upstairs in her room with her best friend, not doing summer reading that is due in two days but loudly laughing or screaming every so often. Both of my kids are wonderful, loving humans. I am grateful for many things in my life, but I am probably most grateful that I have the privilege of knowing these two. I am beyond proud of what genuinely nice people they both are. Are they perfect? Of course not. But they are pretty great, and that's despite all of the mistakes I made along the way, so hurray for that! But let's go back to those mistakes.

## The Pain of Motherhood

You know better than anyone that the journey to even figuring out that your child struggles with anxiety is not easy. The first signs I had were when my daughter couldn't make it through an hour-long church service in the church nursery without crying— scratch that—*screaming* the entire time. Those sweet nursery attendants wouldn't call me, but when I would pick her up, she would be covered in red splotches, the tell-tale sign that she had been crying non-stop. From the very beginning, she didn't like new places or new people. She didn't like change. She took time to warm up to new situations, and as she grew older, she was only willing to try new things if she had a friend.

One of my biggest mistakes was just taking far too long to recognize all of those signs were pointing to her struggle with anxiety. I have a Ph.D. in psychology. I taught child development. I should have seen it. You have no idea the shame and guilt I have wallowed in as I look back at things in hindsight and realize it was anxiety. If you have regrets and beat yourself up about things you didn't realize were anxiety, well I hope you can take a little comfort in knowing that you aren't alone there. I am right there with you, new friend.

One reason it took me so long just to see the anxiety for what it was is that I was always of the "push through" mentality. My wise older sister says her family motto is "suck it up." And maybe deep down, I had the same motto too. When my daughter struggled to adjust each year to a new teacher and a new class of kids, I told her to push through. When she was afraid to go to dance class, it was "push through." When she didn't want to try something new, it was "push through." You get the picture.

I pushed and pushed and pushed that child, and in some respects, pushing was the right thing to do. She knows how to dance and swim and read because I pushed and pushed and pushed some more. I don't know if we could have gotten through those milestones without pushing. And my intention was always, *always* to show her that I had faith in her. I knew she could do it. I hoped she would go into adulthood with some basic faith in herself because she saw her mom always believed she could do it.

However, I still regret that the pushing invariably involved yelling and crying and tantrums sometimes from my sweetie but also sometimes from me. As I have continued down this parenting journey, I have softened quite a bit, and I'm glad about that. One thing I've realized is that it doesn't have to be so hard. Having a child with anxiety wasn't what made it hard. It was *me*. It was how I reacted to her. My methods were wrong. They did achieve results, so I kept using them, but in hindsight, I know there was a better way to achieve those results.

**Perfectly Imperfect, Just Like You**

I know I'm not a perfect mom. This isn't one of those books that you will throw against the wall when you get tired of reading about someone who's never screwed up. On a recent night out with my life-long friends, I was sharing a story, and at the end, we raised a glass to C+ parents. None of us gave ourselves an A or even a B. Prepare yourself. Some of my stories might make you cringe. But as Brene Brown says, "Shame thrives in the dark," so I'm throwing the light on the good, bad, and ugly of my own parenting journey in hopes that you will feel better about your own.

I try not to beat myself up too much about my screw-ups. I try to use the Maya Angelou quote "When you know better, you do better" as my mantra and just do better now because I know better. And that finally gets me to why I wanted to sit down and have coffee with you here today.

I learned some things that changed my life, and as I changed myself, I changed how I parented. And as I changed how I parented, everything started to change. My interactions with my daughter became calmer. And if there is one thing that always helps manage anxiety, it's calmness. Sounds simple, maybe obvious, but I'm here to tell you that some simple, obvious things are a lot harder than they appear. Ever had someone tell you to calm down when you were freaking out? Sounds simple. But did it work? If it was simple, I wouldn't be writing this, and you wouldn't be reading it!

Anyway, another interesting thing happened on my journey. As I finally realized that anxiety was a significant issue that wasn't going away and as I started using every tool I had ever learned in psychology and in all of my years of coaching, figuring out which ones seemed to help, something else started to happen. Although I wasn't doing any sort of marketing, I found I had several clients who were also struggling to parent their anxious children. You could say that is because anxiety is so very common, but I also believe that God sent those clients to me for a reason. My clients helped me figure it out and made me work even harder to find tools and techniques that made parenting beautifully perfect, anxious children easier.

Oh, and I may bring up God a few times in the book. If you use another word for God like Spirit, the Universe, or Allah, please feel free to insert your word in place of the one I use. And if you aren't sure about the whole God thing, that's OK too. You don't have to believe what I believe to get something out of this book. Just know that I believe, and my belief in God has been really helpful when times were the toughest.

So now I want to share the things I've learned with you. I want your parenting journey to be a thousand times easier than mine was. I want you to have some tools to help manage your sweetie pie's anxiety, and I want you to have them a lot sooner and to use them with more ease than I did. I want you to feel great about yourself and your amazing child because we both know that both you and your kid are amazing. And even if you doubt yourself sometimes, I know you're a great mom. I know you're a better mom than I was. And with that as our starting point, you are going to rock this!

If you need another cup of coffee or maybe a snack, go grab one. Then let's get started!

# CHAPTER 3

# Here's Where We're Going and Where We're Going to End Up

L et's get down to business. Is it just me or does saying, "Let's get down to business" always make you think of that song from Mulan, too? Anyway. I digress. But seriously, I do want to get down to business. I am dying to jump in and talk about what we are going to cover and how to get the most out of this book.

## A Quick How-To

If you want to get the most out of this book, start with Chapter 4. There's some foundational stuff in there that I will refer to in almost every other chapter. Specifically, I'm going to try to convince you that anxiety is normal. I know it might be a hard sell, but just hear me out. And then I will discuss painful thoughts, where they come from, and how we get rid of them.

In Chapter 5, I talk about judgment, something we've all experienced, unfortunately. When your child doesn't always act the way other people expect him or her to act, we feel judged. This chapter digs into how to get through those hard times when you feel like someone is judging you or your child

Next, I tackle all of the advice. In Chapter 6, I'll cover some tips for sifting through all of the advice you get from "experts," well-meaning friends and family, and even random strangers who may or may not be so well-meaning.

Chapter 7 focuses on getting and staying calm because when you are dealing with anxiety; the calm has to start with you. Like I said before, lots of things that sound easy aren't, and staying calm in the face of anxiety is still one of the hardest things for most parents—and certainly for me—to do.

In Chapter 8, I invite you to take staying calm one step further by discussing coping strategies and how to get through the toughest times.

And because no one can do this alone, Chapter 9 discusses how to create a support system that really supports you. I know that sounds redundant, but as we'll discuss, sometimes we don't realize that the people we are relying on don't really have our back or give us the real help that we need. The focus of this chapter is to help you identify the people who make it better not worse.

Once you've gone through all of the steps, I'll discuss how to put them together in Chapter 10, and in Chapter 11, I'll show you the ways parents can go wrong.

But that's not all! I said I want this to feel like we are sitting down talking. I use a lot of the same information I'll be sharing with you in this book in a group program that I describe as a cross-between a podcast where you get information and the best parts of a sleepover where you can hang out with cool parents, be real, and share. It's hard to completely recreate that vibe on the written page, but my goal is to try to get there as much as I possibly can.

One way I hope to make this feel like you're chatting with another parent who has been there and knows what your life is really like is by giving you recipes. You might be saying, "Wait, what??" No, this isn't a cookbook, and I am definitely not a chef. However, I am a mom who had days when I was so overwhelmed by my life that the thought of coming up with one more dinner idea felt like it might crush my soul. If you've ever felt that way too, I feel you, sister. And so, I've also somewhat randomly included a few of my favorite go-to recipes in a book about managing your child's anxiety. The recipes are two-for-one recipes because the only thing better than knowing what I am making for dinner one night a week is knowing what I am making on two nights.

So, let's get started, new friend. And as you read, try to imagine me sitting across from you cheering you on. Because I totally am cheering you on. You rock! You're an awesome mom! You got this!

# CHAPTER 4:

# It's All Normal—We Just Don't Think It Is

This anxiety thing is a vicious circular trap. Our kids feel it; we feel it; then our kids feel what we are feeling, and that makes them feel worse, which makes us feel worse. Ugh! Just ugh! So, here's some good news: evolution, natural selection, and survival of the fittest. In my opinion (and if you dig around, I am sure there has to be some data to back me up here), these scientific concepts are one big reason why anxiety is around today and is really only to be expected.

Think of it this way: thousands of years ago, when humans were wandering around in the jungles with no freezer at home filled with DiGiorno's rising crust pizzas or whatever you love, everyone knew that they'd better find something to eat or they were going to go hungry and possibly starve to death. Our jungle ancestors also knew that there were lots of other creatures in that jungle that were facing the same "find something to eat or go hungry and starve" issue. Each day, our ancestors probably faced fairly even odds of eating or being eaten.

So, let's just take two imaginary jungle ancestors as examples to illustrate my theory. Here we have Og and Gog. Og is anxious as all get out. He wakes up every morning terrified of starving to death. Because he is so worried, he gets up before everyone else in the tribe and starts hunting. He also is so nervous that he is totally in tune with everything around him. He notices the weather, the smells in the air, the sounds in the jungle. Oh my goodness, does he ever notice the sounds. He climbs a tree and hides every time he hears a twig snap.

And then there's Gog. Gog is so chill. He was a surfer dude before surfing was even invented. Gog sleeps later than anyone else. When he wakes up, he eats whatever scraps others might have left lying around since everyone else started hunting hours ago. And when Gog finally gets around to hunting, he doesn't get freaked out every time he hears a noise. He takes it in stride. He looks around. He stays calm.

So how does this work out for our friends Og and Gog? Well, Og avoids being eaten because he's so hypervigilant and hides when he hears anything that sounds like it might be a bigger or more vicious predator than he. Og also doesn't starve to death because he spends so much time hunting. He is so focused on every little detail. He notices when it hasn't rained. He notices when seasons are changing. He learns to anticipate and plan for hard times. Not going hungry and the ability to plan ahead makes Og more desirable to the ladies in the tribe than the Bachelor at a rose ceremony. The chicks are all over him, if you know what I mean. So, Og ends up with a very large brood of little Ogs, and most of them inherit his super anxious and hypervigilant tendencies.

And Gog, well our friend Gog obviously didn't fare so well. He tended to go hungry, *a lot*. He was super thin, which might be great if you are walking the catwalk, but not so great if you are trying to survive in the jungle. Being hungry made poor Gog less coordinated and slow. When that hungry lion stumbled upon Gog, he didn't even make a great meal, but the lion was hungry and couldn't pass up such an easy target as was the slow, uncoordinated Gog. Being thin and hungry didn't make Gog very popular with the ladies. No one wanted to snuggle in his tent. Gog became a lion's dinner—well, dinner might be a stretch. He was more like a snack. But he was lion chow before he ever knew the joy of fatherhood. Gog's relaxed, calm genes were not passed on to any offspring.

So, from an evolutionary standpoint, this anxiety your child is experiencing now was a huge biological gift for generations and generations of humans. Your sweet baby's little easily stimulated brain would have kept them alive and well-fed in the jungle long after Gog had met his untimely end. And it's not just the jungle. The humans who totally freaked out and ran when they saw the Viking boats approaching the shore or were terrified and stayed away from that sickly-looking traveler in the middle ages or were too uncomfortable speaking to strangers to mention to the priest that they had doubts about this new religion the king has adopted, those people lived because their anxious thoughts kept them safe.

So here we are today, thankfully in a world where we aren't in danger of being eaten by lions or invaded by Vikings or contracting the bubonic plague. However, we are still the recipients of genetic material from all of those generations of ancestors who lived thanks to their overly-anxious minds.

When you think about it this way, it almost makes you feel like your anxious kid might actually be superior to those genetic freaks of nature who can stay calm all of the time, doesn't it? OK....in fairness, I have to admit that one of my children has always been one of those "freaks" who has this amazing ability to be even-keeled. Obviously, I'm being sarcastic when I say one temperament is superior to another. But in all seriousness, if there is only one thing you get out of reading this book I hope it will be this: your anxious child is *completely normal!* There is nothing wrong with your baby, your sweetie, your little love. I mean it. You may want to argue with me on this. I know I didn't see how they screamed when you dropped them off at preschool or how terrified they were of their first dance recital. I know you are thinking, "But what about the time when…?" Just stop right there. Remember Og and Gog. Og survived because he was more anxious than Gog. Hypervigilance, super-awareness of everything around you, and the tendency to avoid conflict and hide are all human survival skills honed over thousands of years. It's all normal.

An anxious brain is a normal brain. Are there all sorts of variations of normal? Yes, of course. Are some kids more anxious than others? Well, duh! I wouldn't be writing this, and you certainly wouldn't be wasting your time reading it if that wasn't true. However, just because your child falls on a higher end of a continuum and even if your child is so far to the anxious end of the continuum that they need medication to adjust to life in this generation without tigers and Vikings and the plague, your child is still your beautiful, special, wonderful, "normal" kid.

Anxiety is a normal thing in the human population. I am going to keep saying this, and you're going to get sick of me saying this. But as I said, it's really the most important thing in here, so if you want to stop reading, check the box, and say "Got it," I'm OK with that.

If, however, you want to know a bit more about how to best manage your beautiful, sweet, perfect, normal, anxious child, keep on reading because I actually have quite a bit to say about that too.

**Your Sticky Painful Thoughts**

Thoughts, thoughts, thoughts... ever stop to think about just how many thoughts you have? It's constant. From all of the things you need to remember, the snap judgments you make about people and situations, reading between the lines, assessing how this is like that, and figuring stuff out. Unless you are a Zen master who has learned to detach from your thoughts (and if you are, why the heck are you reading this??), the only time you aren't really having thoughts is when you are asleep—and even then you probably dream, so...

Here is a concept that completely blew my mind the first time that I really considered it: not every thought is true. And I don't mean like you made an error solving a math problem so what you thought was the answer isn't true. But what I mean is the thoughts you have like "My child is not normal" or "No one will ever like me if I do X" or "My parents never really loved me." Those thoughts may not be true. Just because you think them—and you might think them over and over and over again—does not make them true.

What thinking them over and over and over again does do, however, is create a very persistent and sticky thought. Now, this is not just my opinion. It's based on actual science and has to do with the way our brains develop. In a nutshell, as our brains develop, the things we think about over and over (and the way we do things) create neural pathways. There is a positive feedback loop in creating neural pathways. The more you do or think something, the stronger the pathway. The stronger the pathway, the easier it is to use the pathway. The easier it is to use the pathway, the more likely you are to use it. And the more likely you are to use the pathway, the stronger it gets. You get the picture.

Strong neural pathways are why it's so hard to write with your non-dominant hand for example. If you have spent twenty or thirty or more years creating a right-handed neural pathway, that left-handed neural pathway doesn't exist, and you will feel like a kindergartner holding a big fat pencil for the very first time when you try to create it. Not to say it isn't possible because it is. Our brains are pretty amazing things.

But just because creating new neural pathways is possible doesn't mean it's easy. And you should never underestimate the human being's desire to avoid doing difficult things and discomfort at any cost. We hate being uncomfortable. Trying to create new neural pathways is uncomfortable. Super uncomfortable.

Especially when you already have these nice comfortable pathways already there. They are so easy to use. It's so much easier to write with your dominant hand. And it's easy to just keep thinking those thoughts that you've thought forever—even if they aren't true or aren't serving you anymore.

So, what does all of this info about neural pathways have to do with how I'm feeling, you might ask. Well, when it comes to the crappy way you are feeling every time you think about your child's struggles with anxiety, your neural pathways have everything to do with it.

**What Do Thoughts Have to Do with the Way You're Feeling?**

Instead of continuing to drone on and on with a boring science lecture, here's a little exercise instead. Start by thinking about a recent difficult experience you've had with your child related to her anxiety. Maybe it was a tough day at school. Maybe it was a terrible playdate. Maybe it was social anxiety. It doesn't matter what you pick. If you're reading this, I am confident you can come up with something.

This part isn't particularly fun, but I'm going to ask you to stick with me. It will get better. Grab a sheet of notebook paper or printer paper or lovely stationery, whatever you've got, and write about that situation. Write out what happened in as much detail as you can. Include sensory information—what did you see, hear, taste, feel. Go write, and when you are done, come back and read the rest.

Ha! I know you're trying to avoid writing about that awful experience and just keep reading, but I'm serious. Go write it down!

OK, I'm trusting you here. Pinky swear that you wrote something.

So now that you relived that incident, write down how you were feeling. Write down your emotions. Were you mad, sad, glad, afraid? And also, write down the physical sensations you were having in your body. Did you start to sweat? Was your face hot? Did your stomach hurt? Did you feel a knot somewhere in your shoulders or neck? Was there muscle tightness in your eyebrows, face, shoulders, or back? Really get granular here, and write everything down.

Now that you are really in tune with everything you were feeling, try to identify what you were thinking. Write down the thoughts that were going through your mind. For example, "This is so embarrassing" or "They will never invite my child over again" or "Why does it have to be so difficult?" or "No one else has to go through this to get their child to attend a birthday party." Write them down. Write as many as you can remember.

Now read over that list of thoughts slowly. Notice how you feel in your body as you read each one. Notice if there is one particular thought that creates a stronger physical reaction than the others. If there is more than one, read them again, and see if there is one that seems to feel the worst. If you are struggling to identify the one single worst-feeling thought, just pick one of the top worst-feeling thoughts and use that one for the rest of this exercise.

Read that thought out loud to yourself once more and, again, feel how the thought makes you feel in your body. Now ask yourself, "What am I making that mean?" and keep asking that question until you feel like you've really gotten to the root of the issue. If that feels too weird or lengthy or like a therapist, just say "So?" after each thought and then answer. Think of it as if you are having a conversation with yourself, and by asking "What am I making this mean?" or just "So?" repeatedly, you will force yourself to dig deeper and deeper into what you are really thinking.

For example, if my terrible thought was "They will never invite my child over again." I would ask myself, "What am I making that mean?" or "So?" And the answer might be that "now my child won't be friends with Bobby anymore."

This may feel a bit repetitive, but thoughts are tricky things, and you will have to ask yourself, "What am I making *that* mean?" or just "So?" quite a few times before you really get to the heart of the matter.

Going back to the example, my response to my terrible thought was "Now my child won't be friends with Bobby anymore." So, I would ask again, "So?" And then I might respond, "Well, if my child isn't friends with Bobby anymore, she won't have a friend in her class." And, then I might ask myself, "What am I making that mean?" And my response might be "If my child doesn't have a friend in her class, she will be socially isolated and alone."

"*So?*"

"If my child is socially isolated and alone, she will never learn how to make friends and will always be socially isolated and alone."

"So?"

"My child will never have any friends."

In this example, you can see how as you dig deeper, it feels as if you are getting closer and closer to the real issue and the real fear that is creating the pain. Never being invited over again really isn't the end of the world, but never having friends is a pretty terrible possibility.

Have you figured out your terrible sticky thought? The thought at the heart of all of those terrible feelings you described at length? I've heard parents say things like "My child isn't normal" or "I am not equipped to handle a child like this, and I will always fail at parenting" or "If I would have done something different years ago, my child wouldn't have these problems now." Those are just a few examples. You may be thinking something else, but whatever you come up with, go ahead and write it down (don't worry, you can burn this when you're done if you want to).

**Your Own Painful Thought**

Now, close your eyes and take five deep belly breaths. Don't cheat. Just do it.

When you are done breathing, take a minute to feel into your heart center, that spot in the middle of your chest that feels like it might burst when your child does something really amazing or sweet. This is a place of deep knowing. When you can tap into this spot, you can circumvent all of that old, powerful neural wiring I went on and on and on about before.

So, as you are breathing and feeling into your heart, I want you to read your terrible thought one more time (and it's better if you can actually say it out loud). Now still feeling into your heart, ask yourself, "Is it true?" Your well-developed neural pathway might try to chime in here and say "Ab-so-freaking-lutely! It *is* true. You know it's true. You have been thinking this for days (or maybe months or even years.) Don't you try to start questioning this really awesome neural pathway you've got going here now!" But stick with it. Take another breath. Close your eyes and feel into your heart and ask again, but this time say, "Can I really absolutely without any shadow of a doubt know that it's true?" and feel into it. Does it feel true?

**You Can't Predict the Future**

So many of our terrible sticky thoughts are about the future, and I have bad news for you. I don't care how smart you are; you don't know what's going to happen in the future. We love to pretend as if we do. But really, we just don't. I could write another long, boring, sciencey paragraph about how our brains only focus on experiences we were right in predicting and ignore all of the times we were wrong so we become convinced we are like the Great Kreskin and can predict everything. But, alas and alack, you cannot. So even without all of my life-coachey voodoo of feeling into your heart, if your terrible thought was about the future, this means you cannot know if it's true. You don't know what's going to happen tomorrow, much less for the rest of your child's life. So get over yourself!

But even if you weren't trying to predict the future, this technique—feeling into your heart, trying to work around those powerful but often incorrect neural pathways, and asking if you really know if the thought is true—can bring relief. And that's what we're after here. I didn't come up with this technique. It's based on *The Work* by Byron Katie. She's written a bunch of books and has a website and an app devoted to *The Work*. If you are interested in really digging into this technique and learning more, go to www.thework.com.

But even if you never learn more than this super simple basic version of *The Work*, you might be amazed, as I was, with the relief that can be found by simply taking the time to figure out what you're thinking that's causing you to feel so bad. And after you take the time to nail down your most painful thought, you can ask yourself if it's true.

More often than not, even if you can't say for certain that the thought you're having isn't true, you will have to acknowledge that you just don't know. If you don't know, there's definitely a possibility that the terrible sticky thought isn't true after all.

## Why It's Important to Start Here

I started by talking about the vicious circle that anxiety can be. It feels bad, so you feel bad, which makes it feel worse and so on and so on. My hope is that this simple tool can help you start to step out of that vicious circle more quickly and just feel better. That's why this chapter comes first.

Before you can even start focusing on practical stuff like creating a support group or determining which advice to take, you need a tool to break the anxiety cycle. And as Gandhi said, "You must be the change you wish to see in the world." As much as we all wish we could wave a magic wand and "fix" other people, you really can't. But you can fix you.

As much as I hate the very tired and overused "put on your own oxygen mask first" analogy, it's tired and overused because it's true. This technique is how you start to put on your own oxygen mask. As you start noticing your thoughts and then questioning them, you will find you are better able to stay present in the moment and react to what is happening right here and now without all of the extra overwhelming baggage of making what's happening right here and now mean something even more terrible. A bad playdate starts to just be that, a bad playdate, not a prediction of unending doom until the end of time.

Step away from the unending doom. Doesn't that feel better?

# CHAPTER 5:

# Deal with the Haters: Handling Judgment

I hope you stuck with me through the last chapter because questioning your painful thoughts is one of the best tools around to help you work through those tough times. Believe me, I've had them too— lying in bed questioning myself, wishing I had done something differently, hating myself for something I said or didn't say or the way I reacted. Anytime you feel that way is the time to jump back to Chapter 4 and dig into what's going on by honestly asking yourself, "What am I making this mean?" And when you get to the heart of the matter, ask, "Do I know for sure it's really true?"

But I know what you're thinking right now. Sometimes, it doesn't really feel like your thoughts are the problem. Sometimes it's everyone else. It's the judgey comments from your mother or your mother-in-law. It's the snide remarks from complete strangers, people who see a tiny snippet of your life and suddenly they think they know what's going on and feel like they have a right to share their opinion with you, people who think your child's panic attack is something you can just discipline away like if you had set stronger boundaries or made them take naps or fed them better food, somehow all of your child's issues with anxiety would magically disappear.

I have been there, believe you me. I will never forget a particularly bad moment after riding the Pink Pig, a Christmas staple in Atlanta. But I digress.

So, yeah. Sometimes people really are judgmental. Sometimes they are mean. And sometimes they're genuinely trying to help but the things they say or the way they say it still makes you feel terrible. What do you do then?

### It's Not You, It's Me

Well, I hate to say this, but even when it really is them and not you, the first thing to do is to go back to the technique we went through in the last chapter and ask yourself, "What am I making this mean?" I know, I know. You want me to say "punch them in the nose" or "give them a piece of your mind." But really, those things won't help, and 99.999 percent of the time, it really isn't what the person said that's the problem. It's what you are making it mean.

I feel your resistance to this through my keyboard. "It's not me; it's them!!" You're screaming. OK. OK. OK. I hear you. Just humor me. Go through the exercise just once and see what happens.

Did you do it? If you did and you were able to see that you were making it mean something that wasn't necessarily true, congratulations! Great job. You may have to remind yourself that your sticky terrible thought isn't true many more times, but with practice, it will start to lose its hold on you.

Because the thing is that while we don't always get to choose our circumstances, we always get to choose how we think about those circumstances. In other words, you don't get to choose whether Billy's mother clutches her pearls when your sweetie pie has a meltdown at Billy's birthday party and says, "My son *never* behaves like that!" However, you do get to choose whether you believe that Billy's mother clearly thinks you are failing as a parent, that you are a big loser in general, and that it will be all your fault when your sweetie pie ends up in jail someday. Or you can choose to believe that Billy's mother is very lucky to have never experienced life with an anxious child yet. We hope for her sake she never does. But if she does, we hope we will show her compassion because we know how terrible it feels when someone judges us.

If thinking kind thoughts and wishing nothing but the best for Billy's judgey mom makes me sound as if I am some sort of saint, I can assure you that is very far from the case. I haven't always chosen option B. I haven't always walked away thinking sweet thoughts and wishing the best for the judgey people in my life. I have no idea who that woman who was horrified by my sweet baby's meltdown at the Pink Pig was, but I assure you my thoughts about her were not kind at all. But here's the weird paradoxical thing I have learned over years and years of feeling judged and then hating myself and hating the person who I thought judged me: it feels a whole lot better when you can break the cycle. I'm not really doing it for them. I'm not choosing compassion because I am a saint. I am choosing it because it makes me feel better.

### What If I Believe It Really Is True?

"Yak, yak, yak," you say. "That's all well and good," you say. "But, I mean it here. This really isn't about my thoughts. This really is about *them*!!"

Alright, already. I hear you. Of course, there are times when someone says something to you that you just can't move past. You may try with your whole heart to go through my little exercise in Chapter 4, but at the end of the day, you are convinced that the sticky terrible thought at the heart of all of your anger or pain really is true. What if you believe your mother-in-law's observation that you aren't doing a great job creating a sleep schedule? You're also annoyed that she chooses to bring it up at every single family dinner. But deep down, you agree with her. Or that annoying neighbor who keeps telling you that you made a terrible mistake years ago; if you just would have quit your job and kept your sweetie pie out of daycare, you wouldn't be having these issues now. What if you think she's right?

That happens sometimes. And when it does, here's what I recommend you do next: Look at that painful thought and determine if your thought relates to anything in the past or in the future. Remember what I said in Chapter 4? We all think we have amazing abilities to predict the future, but we just don't. This is another very sticky thought that you just have to keep tackling over and over and over again. For example, imagine someone tells you repeatedly, "If your sweetie doesn't get into Mrs. Greenbaum's first grade class, your sweetie will be doomed for life." And because that person told you—and maybe "everybody" tells you— you start to believe it's true. And when you use the handy little thought exercise we practiced in Chapter 4 and ask yourself, "Is it true?," you answer hand-over-heart that "Yes! It is absolutely true." Everyone knows Mrs. Greenbaum is the best and any other teacher will be a total and complete disaster." We are going to come back to "everyone" in the next chapter. That's another thought to tackle.

But as you think about your version of Mrs. Greenbaum, I need you to take a breath. Maybe five breaths. Remember, a big part of this exercise is to circumvent all of those persistent neural pathways, and in this case, it sounds like you've built up a nice "Mrs. Greenbaum pathway" that you need to avoid. Feel into your heart. Ask yourself, "Do I really really know that my child's future is doomed without Mrs. Greenbaum? Really, really, do I know that's true?" And if your sticky "Mrs. Greenbaum pathway" refuses to let go, remind yourself, "I do not know what will happen in the future. I do not know what will happen tomorrow, much less how Mrs. Greenbaum or anyone else will impact my sweetie pie."

Same goes for the past. I mean, obviously, you do know what happened in the past. What you do not know, however, and truly will never know is what might have happened if something had been different in the past. This is another favorite painful thought in parenting, one I have been guilty of many, many times. The thought usually starts like this: "If I just hadn't....." For example, "If I just hadn't agreed to move right before middle school, my sweetie pie would have never experienced anxiety and all of the problems that resulted from that anxiety." Maybe you have one of these: "If I just hadn't kept working when they were small, everything would be perfect now," or "If I just hadn't quit my job, I could have sent them to a better preschool, and everything would be perfect now." Sometimes, the thought is even more strongly worded. It might sound like, "I never should have…"

or "I should have known better than to…" or "If I was a good parent, I wouldn't have…"

If your thought has any of these elements, if you are beating yourself up over something that happened in the past, you need to hop back up a few paragraphs and take a breath. Take five breaths. Feel into your heart. I know this is repetitive, but because it runs counter to everything you've learned about your thoughts up until now and it really can change the painful moment into a less painful moment, it bears repeating. And (please note, this is the secret to life right here buried sneakily in the middle of a paragraph. You might want to highlight this!) when you learn to change one little thought, moment by moment, you will change your entire life. You will change how you are feeling. You will change how you react to your circumstances. You will change how you react to other people. And you will change how you react to your child. Will it be instant? Of course not! Will you suddenly implement this technique and everything will change tomorrow? Definitely not! But as Martha Beck describes in *The Four Day Win,* our lives are like the journey of a ship across an ocean. Changing the course by one degree will not seem to make a difference one way or another over a very short distance. However, over time, that one tiny degree of difference will result in reaching a dramatically different destination. That's how life works, folks!

OK, enough about the secret of life and back to those judgey comments. If you were paying close attention to my list of painful thoughts that you might believe are true, you probably noticed one of them was not set in the past or the future. It was the example about sweetie pie needing a better sleep schedule. So, what do you do when someone is giving you judgment and it makes you feel terrible and then you think about it and you feel worse because you agree with it?

Well, in this case, you'll need to add a couple more questions to your list. For the sake of illustration, I'll continue with this scenario: sweetie pie needs a better sleep schedule. I have failed at creating a sleep schedule. It's true. I believe it's true. I really, really know it's true. Now what?

Now you need to ask yourself, "Is this something I can control?" If you live next door to a firecracker manufacturing plant and firecrackers are tested at random times each day, you may not be able to control when sweetie pie takes a nap. Obviously, this is a silly example, and even in the example, I suppose you could move, but the point is there really are times when we are going to experience painful thoughts about things over which we really have no control. And when that happens, the only option we have is to turn that over to a higher power and move on.

**Wait, What??**

"A higher power?" you say. "Is she kidding here?"

Have you ever wondered why there are eight million posters and wall hangings and those old-fashioned dish towels embroidered with the serenity prayer? Here's my guess. It's because having the serenity to accept what we cannot change is freaking hard! So hard that countless generations have written down a prayer and appealed to their higher power to help them do it. So, if you already have a relationship with your higher power—I don't care if you call it God, Jesus, Krishna, Buddha, Allah, the Force, the Universe—now is the time to ask for help. Call your higher power what you will. The point is that when you're able to do this, it's a lot like changing your thoughts. When you turn the things over which you have absolutely no control of to something outside of yourself and let them go, it can be life changing.

But what if you don't have any sort of relationship with any sort of higher power besides your boss and the electric company? What if you actually have resistance to the entire idea of a higher power? Well, if you don't have a relationship with any sort of higher power, I encourage you to try to soften your stance on this just a bit. Think about all of those people who have successfully used twelve-step programs to conquer demons, and try to think, "Well, why not?" Try it out as an experiment. Approach it with curiosity or simply by saying, "I don't really believe in this, but I am willing to give it a shot and see what happens."

One technique for turning things over that I have found especially helpful both for believers and non-believers is to create a God box. A God box is simply a box of your choosing where you physically put your cares in order to give them to your higher power. I personally like boxes with a lid. There is something very satisfying in putting something in a box then closing the lid on it. However, you can create whatever system works for you. I suppose you could have a God envelope if that floats your boat. My God box is a small heavy cardboard box that once held a necklace I had ordered online. I found a picture of an angel statue on the internet, printed it, and taped it over the jewelry logo to make it feel more "Godly." I use it when I am facing something that is completely out of my control, something I need to turn over to God. I simply write the problem on a small slip of paper and put it in the box.

I also have a practice of opening the box every three months or so to remove anything that is no longer an issue. Without getting all religious on you, you would be amazed by how many things I am able to throw away after three to six months. I'm talking about things that were keeping me up at night. Things that felt so heavy and impossible to solve. Things like people because as you know, you can't really control or change other people. So I write their names on a slip of paper and put it in the God Box. And lo and behold, stuff like unsolvable problems with other people often gets resolved, sometimes in ways I would call miraculous, but I won't because I just said I wouldn't get religious!

### It's True, and I Can Control It. What Now?

Back to the decision tree. You've got a thought that you believe is true. We just discussed what to do if the thought is about something that is completely out of your control. However, there are times when you will have a painful thought, and it is within your control to change it. In that case, there is one last question to ask yourself: do I care or am I motivated enough to do something about this? If the answer is no, to the God box it goes. However, I think you know what to do if the answer is yes.

Let me say that in this case, I don't expect for one second that doing something will be easy. If it was easy, you would have fixed it long ago and moved on. Fixing it may require lots of thought, work, money, time, help. Realistically, it will probably require all of the above. You may find it requires you to think strategically or to go back to the drawing board so to speak.

And do you know what I recommend that helps with those really tough issues that you know you need to fix but are hard or expensive or time-consuming or all of the above? You guessed it. Put it in the God box. Just because I am working on something doesn't mean I don't want divine assistance along the way, but maybe that's just me.

So that's it—a formula for dealing with those annoying judgments. It will also help deal with those annoying people who judge. In reading it, it may have felt like there were a lot of steps, but it's actually not too bad when you see them listed one after the other. Here they are in a simple outline format:

How do I deal with judgements from others?

- Question my thoughts. Are they true? Do I really know they are true?
  » If no, I will take a breath and remind myself every time the thought comes up that the thought isn't true.
  » If I believe the answer is yes, they are true, I will ask if this is a thought about what will happen in the future or what might have happened in the past if I had done something differently?
    - If yes, I will remember that I can *never* know what will happen in the future or what might have happened if I did things differently.
    - If no, I will ask myself, "Is this something I can control?"
      » If no, I will turn it over to my higher power and do my best to let it go.

&raquo;  If yes, ask, "Do I care enough about this to do something about it?"

- If no, I will turn it over to my higher power and do my best to let it go.
- If yes, I will dig deep, ask for help, and look at different solutions I haven't tried before. AND I will turn it over to my higher power.

Next time Mary Lou feels compelled to step out of her car in the carpool line to tell you that even though she knows you are trying your best, she really feels you could have handled the distribution of snacks at the class party differently, just flip back to this page and start at the beginning.

You got this.

**But Wait, There's More!**

Because you are doing hard things, I want to share one more thing. It's the proverbial straw that is going to break this mama camel's back: dinner! Are you with me on this? I mean, by the time dinner rolls around, it often feels as if I've already lived a lifetime that day, and the thought of having to come up with something and then cook that something makes me want to cry.

I don't know why, but I feel like you really understand where I am coming from on this. Because

I love you, I am going to randomly share a few of my go-to recipes throughout the book. They all have upsides and downsides—like everything in life, really. But my hope is that in addition to all of the really cool techniques and the secret of life, these recipes will make your life a little easier.

Here we go.

## Dual-Purpose Roasted Chicken
### *Ingredients:*

- 1 whole chicken. The biggest whole chicken you can find—if you are a stickler about organic free-range, you might actually want to get two chickens as they tend to be smaller. Just make sure you have a roasting pan big enough to fit whatever you buy.
- 1 to 2 lemons
- Several springs of fresh Rosemary
- Garlic. I use pre-minced in a jar. If you are a purist and want to mince your own, I won't stop you, but the pre-minced works just fine in my opinion.
- Kosher salt
- Pepper
- Olive oil
- Green tabasco (optional)
- Small potatoes and an onion (optional)

- Premade, refrigerated tortellini—I think the cheese-stuffed are the most kid-friendly, but you know your kids. If they'll eat mushrooms or sundried tomatoes, go for it.
- Premade refrigerated pesto

You may have noted that there are no measurements above like a teaspoon or ¼ of a cup. Technically, this isn't that kind of recipe. I sort of make it up as I go and that makes it very easy to adjust to your own family's taste. For example, if you hate rosemary, that's cool. Just leave it out.

### Instructions

You want to prep the chicken either the night before you want to cook it or at least the morning before you plan to have it for dinner. Also, please note because this is a biggie, this chicken takes two hours to cook. If that is a non-starter for a weeknight meal because you are never home early enough to spend two hours cooking before everyone in your house dies from starvation, I hear you. Just prep the chicken on Saturday, put it in the fridge, and cook it for dinner on Sunday night. Then use the leftovers to make chicken pesto pasta for dinner on Monday or Tuesday night. Getting two dinners out of one "thing" is pure gold in my book, and it's why I'm sharing this recipe with you here. So, let's do this.

To create your seasoning rub, you want to make enough of this to put beneath the skin of the entire chicken and inside the cavity. In a small bowl, pour in a healthy portion of salt. I probably use around a half cup. I know that seems outrageous, but you would be hard-pressed to find something that is "too salty" for me. So, if that seems a step too far, take it down to a ¼ cup. Next, add your pepper. Again, this is to your taste. My kids aren't big pepper fans, so I probably use around a tablespoon. Some people use the half-as-much-pepper-as-salt rule, so if that isn't too peppery for you, go with that. Adjust it to your taste. Add the zest of the lemon and all of the juice. Just like salt, I love garlic, so I add two big healthy tablespoons. Let your conscience be your guide. Then the rosemary. I wash it, pull the leaves off the stem and either cut them with scissors or chop it with a knife. Either way works. I suppose you could even skip chopping and put the rosemary leaves in whole, but I think you get more flavor if you chop it up. Something about releasing the oils, but I'm no chef, so who knows? Then I add a bit of olive oil—probably around a tablespoon. If I'm in the mood or if I remember, I might add some green tabasco.

The beauty of this is you really can't screw it up. You may make it and think, "I'll add more salt next time" or whatever, but I've probably made this chicken a hundred times, and this recipe has never let me down. And in all those times, I've never measured an ingredient. Not once!

After you create your rub, get ready to put it on the bird. Start with two large pieces of aluminum foil. Both pieces should be large enough to wrap completely around your chicken. Position the foil in a cross or X and place your chicken in the middle. (Don't forget to take any giblets out of the cavity of the chicken before you start. My mom used those parts to make gravy but they kind of creep me out, so I always throw them away.) Now this part is a little gross but totally worth it. You have to separate the skin from the meat of the chicken. Just work it with your hands, sliding your fingers beneath the skin as far around as you can. If you can, get down by the thighs and even separate the skin from the drumsticks. Now just use your hands to apply your salt rub mixture to the meat of the chicken beneath the skin. Be generous. Put it everywhere you can reach and rub some inside the cavity of the chicken. I usually put a whole spring of rosemary inside the chicken. If I have another lemon, I cut it up and put it in there too. Sometimes I throw a bit of onion in there. If you have salt rub left after you have coated beneath the skin and the cavity, rub it on the outside of the skin too.

When your chicken is fully covered in your rub, wrap it securely in foil then place the foil-wrapped chicken in one (or two if you are really fastidious) plastic grocery bags. Tie the bags and place the chicken in the fridge until you are ready to cook. If you don't want to spend your time cleaning the juice of raw chicken that dripped and seeped in your fridge, don't skip that bagging step. Trust me on this one.

When ready to cook, preheat your oven and your roasting pan to 375 degrees. (Don't forget, this chicken will need to cook for two hours, so don't forget to plan accordingly. Get this puppy in the oven long before everyone is starving. If you have a little raised wire rack doohickey that fits inside your roasting pan, you will put that in after the pan is preheated.

If you don't have a rack or if you want an easy side that's done when the chicken is done, wash some little potatoes (or cut larger potatoes into chunks). Toss the potatoes with a bit of olive oil. If you like onion, cut up a yellow onion and toss it in there too. Go very easy on salt and pepper because if you used as much salt as I always use, the chicken juices will be salty, and the potatoes will cook in the chicken juice.

Either place your rack in the hot pan or pour the potatoes in your preheated pan, then put your chicken *breast side down* on top. Set your timer for an hour, and go live your best life until the timer goes off. After an hour, flip the chicken over and set the timer for another hour. Depending on the size of your chicken, it may be done a bit earlier, but two hours is a pretty safe bet for a big chicken. If you have a meat thermometer, use it to check for doneness. If you don't, err on the side of cooking longer rather than shorter. The skin should be golden brown, and the meat should be firm, white, and the juices should run clear when the chicken is fully cooked.

In the final hour, you can prep anything else you want to go along with your chicken. Steamed broccoli is my go-to. This roasted chicken should smell great as you are cooking it and will give you a real old-fashioned sit at the table kind of meal.

But here is the real beauty. In a day or so, you can use your leftovers to make another meal. *Yes*! Most of the work is already done, and you don't have to think of something else to make. You are welcome!

**Chicken Pesto Pasta**

One of my kids loves pesto while, of course, the other hates it. So, at my house, I usually reserve some of the tortellini after I drain it, and my anti-pesto kid eats the tortellini buttered as a side with some reserved chicken. You can adapt this recipe easily to your family's taste. Change the sauce, omit the sauce, or create two versions. It's so easy that I don't mind adapting this one for my picky eater.

So, the reason I said get a big chicken or two small chickens is that your goal is to have some leftover chicken. I try to save some breast meat when I roast a chicken because I prefer breast meat in chicken pesto pasta but it really doesn't matter.

## *Instructions*

- Lightly shred the leftover chicken meat into bite-sized pieces and warm it in the microwave.
- Prepare that refrigerated tortellini according to the directions on the package.
- Add the chicken and dump in some pre-made pesto and, voila, dinner number two.

CHAPTER 6:

# Opinions Are Like A*******: What to Do with All of the Advice?

Now that we've tackled handling all of the judgment that gets thrown around, let's talk about a somewhat related topic: advice. In many ways, advice is a blessing, especially as a parent. How many times have you found the perfect place or thing or recipe or technique because someone else gave you their advice?

When my kids were babies, I was in a "playgroup"—shout out to the Kangaroos—and those mamas got me through my first few years of parenting. There was nothing I needed to know that one of them hadn't already figured out or was in the process of figuring out. We shared books, recipes, sleep schedules—for ourselves and our babies—you name it. If somebody asked about it, somebody else had advice. And that advice was what got me through.

But advice also has a dark side. It's often unsolicited, and unsolicited advice can send us into a spiral of self-doubt and recrimination. When anyone suggests how you should change or do things differently, especially if you weren't actually asking for help, it's not uncommon to assume that the only reason anyone would offer advice is that they assume you are doing something wrong. They obviously think you need correcting.

When you start assuming that you know why someone gave you advice, you are often jumping right back into the quagmire that makes you ask, "What am I making that mean?" Once someone throws out even the kindest and most well-meaning advice in the world, it is a very common tendency to make that advice mean something not so great about you.

For example, Mary Lou says, "I think you should take your daughter off of all social media. It's clear she's struggling with social anxiety, and social media just makes that worse." And Mary Lou may not be judging in any way. Mary Lou really might love your daughter and want to offer her help. However, many, if not most, parents on the receiving end of Mary Lou's helpful advice might start to think things like, "Mary Lou thinks I don't know what I'm doing. Mary Lou thinks I am failing my daughter. If I had never let her get Snapchat, this wouldn't be happening now. My daughter's social anxiety is all my fault." And there you go into the dreaded dark spiral of making Mary Lou's comment about social media mean something else, something a whole lot worse, something personal about you and your parenting.

Luckily, from the last two chapters, you're already aware of what to do with those kinds of thoughts. But the dark spiral of painful thoughts isn't the only issue we run into when confronted with advice.

### It's Just So Freaking Overwhelming!!

In addition to jumping to all sorts of conclusions about what Mary Lou *really* meant by her suggestion, advice can also throw us into a complete state of overwhelm about what we actually should be doing to help our child. The title of this chapter is a quote from a Dirty Harry movie—Google it if you're too young to remember Dirty Harry movies—and it goes like this, "Opinions are like a*******; everybody has one." The reason I chose that as the title (besides the fact that it kind of makes me laugh) is because it really sums up how it feels to be the parent of a struggling child. Everybody does seem to have an opinion about what you should do, how you should do it, and what would make things better.

And I'm not even just talking about your friends and family. I'm also talking about your pediatrician, your psychologist, psychiatrist, social worker, parenting expert, parenting magazines, books, websites, email blurbs, Instagram posts, etc. Advice about anxiety seems to be everywhere. And in your desire to do whatever you can to help our children, it is all too easy to find yourself in complete information/advice overload.

Not to mention that sometimes that advice feels as if it's coming from someone who doesn't live in the real world. Have you ever felt like the advice you heard or read would require you to quit your job, ignore your other children and/or spouse, and devote yourself full-time like a monk in monastery to implement this tool or technique that the experts claim will solve everything? I certainly have. I have often found myself lying in bed reading yet another book on how to "fix" my child and getting more and more frustrated because I felt like the author, who claimed to be an expert, just didn't get it. They just didn't know what it was like to do the job and pay the bills and cook the food and do the laundry and quiz the spelling words. I couldn't figure out how I was supposed to also start doing all of the stuff they thought I was supposed to be doing too.

And even if the advice didn't feel overwhelming, I often felt as if it wasn't right for my child. Call it parent's intuition or just that sense of knowing the kid you know better than anyone. Still, there were suggestions that I knew weren't right for the little person in front of me no matter how great they may have worked for other kids.

So what did I do? Actually, I shouldn't even put that in past tense because it still happens all of the time. And when it does, here's what helps me:

## Breathe

The first thing I do when I find myself feeling frustrated or overwhelmed or even sometimes pissed off by advice regardless of whether it comes from my pediatrician or a complete stranger is to breathe. "Are you kidding?" you might be thinking. "Breathe is about as cliché as your earlier suggestion to turn things over to a higher power!" Yeah, yeah, I hear you. But in this case, the advice to breathe really is true and a good one and here's why.

We humans have these amazing brains that can think all of these amazing thoughts. In Chapter 4, you recall we talked about how your thoughts can create emotions and by changing your thoughts about your circumstances you can change how you feel even if your circumstances do not change. That's all true and important stuff, but here is something else to consider. We modern humans also have a tendency to overthink. We over-rely on our clever brains and give too much credit to those thoughts which may not even be true. When we aren't careful, we live our lives inside our heads.

When I force myself to breathe, what I am really doing is trying to step out of my very useful brain and away from all of the thoughts that may or may not be true but in the moment are freaking me out. The act of consciously breathing, not the unconscious breathing you do all of the time, forces your attention on something else, and when you feel overwhelmed or frustrated or angry, that focus on something else is a really good thing. Conscious breathing is slow and deliberate. Sometimes it helps to count to five as you inhale and again as you exhale.

Please note, this little breathing tip is a two-for-one special because once you master the stop and breathe technique, it's a great one to teach—and even more importantly—to model for your anxious child. When your child sees you do this to calm yourself down and sees that it actually works, they are more likely to try it themselves.

Keep in mind, however, that breathing is like a lot of things "everyone" says you are supposed to do like eating nine servings of vegetables a day or meditating. It sounds a lot easier than it really is. Stepping away from your thoughts and focusing on your breath takes practice, and it requires self-compassion because you will forget to do it and then get frustrated with yourself that you reacted without breathing like you meant to.

Beating yourself up for not doing it right is not the way to get better at it. Berating yourself when you forget or feel like you didn't do it right is basically the equivalent of scolding your toddler for falling down when she is learning to walk. It wouldn't have helped her walk better or sooner and probably would have set her back. Same principle applies here.

## Take Your Breathing to the Next Level

One thing that might help you get this technique right more often is to come up with some sort of mantra. A mantra is simply a word or short phrase that's easy to remember and repeat when you need to step away from your thoughts and back into your breath. Mantras can also remind you of something you aspire to or a way you want to be in the world.

I personally like a mantra I got from Gabby Bernstein's book *The Universe Has Your Back*. Berstein says, "I am determined to see this with love." I wrote this phrase on a few little pieces of paper and taped them to my computer and to the back of my phone case. I say it as I slowly inhale and again as I exhale. And I don't just say it when I am frustrated by advice. I also say it when I am stuck in traffic or running late (and that's like *always!*) or annoyed with one of my kids or whenever. Breathing and repeating my mantra can help me get out of my head for long enough to stop spiraling in thought and calm down just a bit.

## Trust Your Gut

Breathing can help get you out of your head. Getting out of your head is the key to dealing with advice frustration and overwhelm. In fact, it's also the key to tuning into your gut/intuition.

When I said above that we modern humans tend to overthink things, what I meant was we tend to believe all problems are meant to be solved with our heads. We've spent years and years in school learning how to use our heads to solve things and to answer questions. So of course, it's our go-to. However, we forget that school as we know it is a relatively modern idea that was created to make good factory workers for the industrial revolution. School was never designed to show us how to tackle life problems such as how to make friends, how to forgive each other, or how to manage our children's apparent addiction to social media.

School has become this common human experience most of us share and understand. So, of course, it makes perfect sense that you have applied the same "school-like" problem-solving technique to everything. But long before humans went to school for years and years, we had another way to make decisions and figure things out. In addition to using our very smart brains, we also trusted our guts.

Modern science has even discovered that there is a real scientific phenomenon behind the phrase "trust your gut." Your gut (technically our gastrointestinal system) is actually far more connected to the brain and, therefore, moods than previously thought. And it isn't a one-way connection. Most people have experienced the ways in which thoughts can impact the stomach like getting "butterflies" or feeling queasy. But your stomach can also impact your brain. (As a side note, there's some really interesting stuff out there about anxiety and gut health. And I say "interesting" only if you are a geek like me who thinks that kind of thing is interesting. Feel free to spend some time searching Google for "gut health and anxiety" but only if you aren't already feeling overwhelmed by "all of the things".)

Your gut is a great source of information when you are able to tune in to it. However, in order to tune into your gut, you need to tune out from your brain, if only temporarily. One way to do this is to use a technique Martha Beck describes in *Finding Your Own North Star* called the body compass. To start using your body compass, you first need to do a quick exercise to get a calibration—that's a fancy way of saying you need to tune into how your gut feels when something is wrong and how it feels when something is right.

Now, this is a simplification, and for a more detailed description, read Martha's book (which is actually a great book anyway and worth a read). First, find a place and time where you can sit in relative peace and quiet for around twenty to thirty minutes. This will probably be easiest to do if you read through it all first, then try to do it.

## Tune into Your Gut

Start by using the breathing techniques I discussed above to help you calm down and get centered with five, long, deep inhales and exhales. Now I know this sounds icky, but I promise it won't last long. Try to remember a time when you made a bad decision. If you can remember a bad decision regarding your child, that's even better. Maybe you pushed them to do something that you wish you hadn't. Maybe you allowed or said yes to something you regret.

When you come up with your bad decision, I want you to remember that moment when you knew without a shadow of a doubt it had been a bad decision. Odds are good that you knew it was bad before something bad had actually happened. You just knew. Try to remember the moment in as much detail as you can. Remember sensory details if you can, like what did you see, hear, feel, etc. Where were you? What was happening around you? Who else was there? When you are fully into the memory of the bad decision, notice your body. Really notice what it feels like in your body. Does your stomach hurt? Does your throat feel tight? What physical sensations do you feel?

One of my many bad decisions was letting my daughter ride her bike down a really steep hill when she was too small, and I should have known she wasn't ready. She fell and still has a scar on her shoulder where she scraped it. I remember there was a moment right before she fell when I knew that I never should have let her ride down that hill. Your body often "knows" things before your brain has had a chance to process what's happening and definitely before you can put it into words. When I think of that instant my body knew before my brain did, my stomach hurts like something is squeezing it from all sides. That is my bad decision gut feeling. Yours is probably not the same as mine, but when you do this exercise, you will start to get a sense of what a bad decision feels like in your gut/body.

Now take a few breaths and actually physically shake off that feeling. I mean it. Stand up and shake, wiggle, stomp. Do whatever it takes until the bad feeling is gone.

Next, switch gears and think about a good decision—something that had real consequences, not just what you decided to have for lunch. Maybe it was a significant financial investment or taking a new job or doing something entirely outside of your comfort zone. If you can think of an example related to your child, even better. Think back to the time you made the decision, before you knew if it would be OK or not—when you pushed the button or walked into the room or when you said "yes." And just like before, try to immerse yourself in what you were seeing, hearing, smelling, or tasting. Remember as much as you can about the experience and when you are really into that moment, feel into your body. You might feel nervousness in your stomach or chest, maybe a sense of excited energy. However, even though the feelings around both your good decision and your bad decision may involve fear, you should be able to notice a difference between how your body felt about the first decision and how it felt about the second decision.

The reason I wanted you to think about decisions that went wrong versus decisions that went well is that there is typically an element of fear with both. Fear is a common element whenever we make decisions regarding our children, but as I hope you felt in this exercise, there is a subtle difference between the fear you feel when something just isn't right and the fear you feel when you are doing something new and different but your gut/body tells you it is the "right" thing to do.

The body sensations you felt as you did this exercise should help you begin to see that your gut/body does tell you things. It gives you clues as to whether you are on the right track or not. The trick is, as I said before, getting out of your head long and often enough to notice what your body is trying to say.

You can use this technique whenever you are trying to figure out if you should accept a particular piece of advice. Try to imagine taking the advice in as much detail as you possibly can and then feel into your body. How does it feel? Heavy? Scary? Scary but in a good way? Exciting? Now imagine the opposite, not taking the advice. How does that feel? I feel like I am really making a habit of exposing the truth behind clichés and common sayings, but here's one more. You know why people say, "When I made that decision, it felt like a weight had been lifted?" Because often when you make a change or decision that you know in your body is the right decision, it feels like a weight has been lifted. Maybe it's off your shoulders or chest, but a heavy feeling goes and is replaced with a lightness.

Learning to tune into and listen to my body is one of the best techniques I know for determining which advice I should take and which I should skip. But here are a few additional things I've learned as I have navigated the advice highway.

## Three More Tips on Advice

### No Technique or Brilliant Piece of Advice Works Every Single Time

There may be exceptions to this but so far, I haven't found one. It's always disappointing when the "thing" I discovered that worked so beautifully once or twice or six dozen times suddenly doesn't work. Maybe it's the situation, or maybe it's just that my child has grown and changed, and it doesn't really apply to what's going on with her anymore. Sometimes, the advice not working is a fluke, and it works again next time. But I find it isn't unusual to need to switch it up and try something new even after I've found something that worked for a while.

### *Give Yourself Permission to Try Things*

Trying things just feels so much less permanent and heavy and overwhelming than committing to a technique, process, or method. If someone suggests something, there's something easy about shrugging your shoulders and saying, "What the heck? I'll try it." And of course, trying means you aren't stuck with what feels like a permanent commitment to something that just doesn't fit with you or your child's personality, lifestyle, temperament, etc.

### *While You're Giving Yourself Permission to Try, Give Yourself Permission to Give Up*

I once had a client who was working with the expert in her community to help her anxious child deal with social issues. Everyone recommended this lady. The expert had a very rigid set of rules you had to follow without exception. And because she was the expert, my client felt like she had to do everything exactly as the expert said, even if it felt wrong in her body or punitive to her child. My client was paying for advice from the expert and then paying me to coach her through the terrible feelings she had about implementing the expert's advice. It was a classic example of trying to ignore what her body was saying to her. The expert's system just didn't work with her or her child's personality, temperament, etc. Just as you must give yourself permission to try, you must also give yourself permission to give up, even when the expert tells you that's what you should never do. Of course, I'm not saying if it feels hard, just give up because we have to do hard things. Parenting an anxious child often feels hard, and you can't ever give up. I'm just saying you should trust your gut. When something really just doesn't feel right, it's OK to not do it, even if an expert or "everyone" says you should.

So there you are. A few tips that I find helpful as I try to manage all of the endless advice that seems to be flying at me from all directions these days. And since we are talking about advice, I thought it might be nice to end with one of the most helpful pieces of advice I've come across that has helped me as a parent of an anxious child. It comes from *Helping Your Anxious Teen* by Sheila Achar Josephs, Ph.D. You probably already know this, but the thing about anxiety is that it often results in your child being completely unwilling to do something that you want or need her to do. In those situations, it's easy for anxiety to create a conflict between you and your sweetie pie. Dr. Josephs recommends that you always keep your focus on how you and your child can work together against anxiety, not how you and your child work against each other. For me, this technique was a lot like Byron Katie's focus on your thoughts—simple but truly life-changing. When I am able to shift from being in conflict with my child to working with her to overcome anxiety, the entire dynamic changes. And with each shift in tone and dynamic, our relationship and our feeling of success as a family increases.

# CHAPTER 7:

# Find Your Calm in the Chaos: Unfortunately, It's Got to Start with You

As I write this, Taylor Swift has just released a new song, "You Need to Calm Down." It's catchy, as are most of Swift's tunes. By the time you read this, there will probably be eight million memes using some line from the song. I should probably be playing it as I write this chapter because if you are the parent of an anxious child, you really do need to calm down.

Anxiety is some powerful stuff, as I'm sure you've noticed. OK, that was a joke. Of course, you've noticed. In my house, we started referring to it as the anxiety train, as in "the anxiety train just blew through." It was not uncommon on a particularly bad day for everyone in my house to get swept up in the wake of the anxiety train. Wait, trains don't have wakes. Whatever. You get what I mean.

With the whole family being impacted by the anxiety train, one key thing I had to figure out in my house was how to keep one person's meltdown from creating a meltdown for the entire family. Now, that might sound easy, but I have a feeling you know, new friend, that it's not as easy as it sounds. In fact, it took me quite a bit of time to achieve. Things did get better in my house. And I know that it wasn't only one thing that created the improvement. Actually, putting in practice the advice and techniques from chapters 4, 5, and 6 certainly had an impact. But there was something else that really seemed to help me create more calm at home. I became a meditator.

I can hear your groan from here. "First, the God box. Then, the breathing and mantras. Now, meditation?!? I did not sign up for this," you say. "I want tips to help my child!" you say. "Why, Tonya, why? Why are you making me do all of this stuff that has nothing to do with my sweetie pie?"

But, alas, what you do has everything to do with your sweetie pie. In terms of creating calm, as difficult as this might be to hear, it has to start with you. I'm sure you've noticed that I just hate the phrase "you have to put on your own oxygen mask first." But as much as I hate that saying, it really is true in every sense that people use it. Parents have to take care of themselves first. And in truth, while meditation is taking care of yourself, your meditation practice can have a profound effect on your anxious child. I sense your skepticism so I'm going to throw some science at you.

## Entra-what?

Entrainment is the name for the phenomenon of things altering their rhythms to be in sync when they are together. (Google "entrainment pendulum" for an example.) There are all sorts of examples in nature. It happens because the things (organisms, people, whatever) expend less energy when they operate in sync than when they operate on different rhythms. In simple terms, it is easier to move at the same pace as everyone/thing around you than to move at a very different pace. So, things (organisms, people) naturally and often unconsciously move to adopt whatever rhythm is the strongest when they come together. Scientists have measured how heart rate and breathing rate changes when people do nothing except listen to different types of music for example. Humans are rhythmic creatures, and we entrain to the world around us and mostly to each other. Ever felt caught up in the frenetic energy of a group who is rushing around and found yourself rushing too?

But the crazy thing about entrainment is it doesn't only happen with rhythms or beats or pace. It also happens with energy or mood and even behaviors. I know you've experienced this too. You've walked into a room where something good or bad has just happened, and you find yourself swept up in the good or bad feelings that surround you. When my daughter was in fourth grade, she suddenly started dressing and wearing her hair like her new best friend. It seemed she was entraining to her friend's style.

Another "natural law" of sorts is that bad tends to be stronger than good. There are lots of examples of this being true. People remember bad things more easily than good things. It takes something like five positive interactions with someone to overcome the effect of one negative interaction. When you took tests in school, you always remembered what you got wrong, but rarely remembered all of the things you got right. In Chapter 4, we talked about how focusing on the bad was key to keeping our ancestor Og alive.

So, if entrainment is a thing, which it is, and if bad is stronger than good, which it is, what do you think that means? It means that when your sweetie pie is melting down, it's easy (one might even say natural and predictable) for that bad energy to sweep up everyone in its path—or in this case, everyone in your family, especially you. I feel pretty comfortable in assuming that you know exactly what I am talking about. You've been there. You've gotten sucked into a terrible mood or into feeling just as anxious and panicked as your child.

And that, my friend, is where meditation comes in. You may think meditation is for hippies or yogis or new-age types. But I'm here to tell you, new friend, if you want a way to learn to control your own energy without entraining to the most negative feeling in the room, meditation is also for you.

## But Meditation Seems So ... (Fill in the Blank)

So before I say anything about how to do it, I think it's important that I spend a few minutes talking about my own struggles with meditation and why it seemed to take forever for me to find a method that worked. I had read and talked to all kinds of meditators over the years and they always seemed to be made of different stuff than I was made of. I would describe myself as more high-strung, more type-A, more foul-mouthed, more sarcastic, and easily annoyed. Meditators always seemed so calm.

So there was my first hang up. I told myself that I wouldn't be good at it. I wasn't the right type of person to do it. But guess what? Those were just my thoughts, and it turns out that like so many other times, my thoughts weren't true. It wasn't until I was able to see that maybe my thoughts weren't true and maybe I was wrong about meditation that I was able to even give it a try.

And that brings me to the second big hurdle I had to overcome to become a meditator. In order to do it and to keep doing it, I had to embrace the concept I introduced in the last chapter when I talked about taking advice. I had to "just try" without being super attached to what that meant. I had to give myself permission to do as much or as little as I wanted and to accept that some days would be better than others. I've had to adopt that same position with running and exercise in general, by the way, because when I had a rigid, "I have to run 3 miles or I won't run at all" position, I never ran at all. When I finally said to myself, "You are allowed to run as far as you want, and you can stop when you want to," I was finally able to run regularly and actually farther than I ever had before. One of my favorite movie lines of all time is "Lighten up, Francis" from *Stripes*. I say it to myself all the time. Sometimes, lightening up on yourself can actually make you more productive, believe it or not.

It took me quite a while, however, to realize that simple fact about lightening up. My first real introduction to meditation was in a free class taught by a master meditator who spent at least an hour each day in meditation and told us he regularly achieved nirvana in these sessions. I am nothing if not a diligent student. This was a class, and the "teacher" had just given us the goal. Therefore, I set out to achieve nirvana (which, in case you're wondering, is the exact opposite of lightening up!). I didn't and still really don't know the precise technical definition of nirvana, but my idea was that it was complete and total enlightenment, absolute calm, and moving to another state of consciousness where nothing, and I mean nothing, could upset me or freak me out.

I tried and tried and tried to achieve nirvana. Like I said, I wasn't really sure what nirvana was, but by golly, I was going to get there. And that white-knuckled trying was exactly the thing that kept me from being a meditator for years. I'd try with the idea that anything less than nirvana was a failure. So, of course, every session was a failure. And failure is disappointing. And it's hard to keep doing something that's just a constant disappointment. I'd start and quit and start again. It wasn't until I was willing to relax and let go of the idea that I had to achieve something—or anything—that meditation seemed to click for me. It was almost like I accepted that I was never going to reach nirvana, and by doing so, I got closer to nirvana than I ever had before. Technically, I'm still not sure that I really know what nirvana is, so who knows if I've achieved it or not? However, what I have achieved is a base level of calm that I can access more easily than I could before I spent hours and hours and hours trying to meditate.

**Embrace the Paradox**

Meditation (and running and really most things in life) is all about accepting and even embracing paradox. Sorry, that probably sounds heavy and complicated, so before you doze off, let me say it in another way. What I had to learn to do was to accept two opposite ideas as being equally true at the same time. Still too complicated? Here's what I mean. My secret to meditation is to show up and do it regularly, and in that sense, I am putting in the effort and trying. But at the same time, my secret to meditation is to show up, not expect anything to happen, and not to try at all but just to do it anyway. It's about doing it and going along with the process without being overly worried about what I am achieving or what's going to happen in the end. Doing it that way is what FINALLY helped me be a meditator. And when I was finally able to just sit down and detach from the millions of random thoughts that bounce around my brain constantly without trying to achieve nirvana or anything else, I started to, as Taylor Swift says, calm down.

Finding calm is my antidote to the scientific fact of entrainment. It is my way of being the strongest energy in the room. Well maybe that's a bit of an exaggeration because, let's face it, the anxiety train is some pretty strong energy. But when I am calm, I at least have a shot at keeping my energy separate from what's happening around me. Do I stay calm and collected every single day without fail? Of course not. I still get caught up most of the time. In the past, however, I always got caught up. So now, every time I don't is an improvement. And just like I'm not trying to achieve nirvana, I'm not trying to achieve perfection—not as a meditator or as a parent or as a human being. After years of trying, I now think achieving perfection and nirvana both are impossible goals, and impossible goals are just big fat bummers.

I hope I've convinced you to "just try" meditating. You don't have to be good at it. You don't have to achieve anything. There are tons of books, videos, and even apps for your phone. Just like you shouldn't try to be perfect when you start meditating, you also shouldn't try to have a perfect meditation practice. There isn't one special way of doing it that works while the other ways are less than. Truly, the secret is to find whatever works for you and just do it as regularly as you can. Do you like guided meditations? Awesome! So do I. Prefer to sit in silence? Cool, me too. Do you like to listen to recordings of weird meditation sounds? Yep, I use those too. Seriously, I do just about every type of meditation that exists depending on where I am, how much time I have, and just how I'm feeling that day. It's all great. It's all better than not doing it. It all will help you stay centered and calm.

And remember what I said about advice—that as you are trying, it's really counterproductive to beat yourself up when you mess up? Well, that's equally true about your meditation practice. Remember the analogy I used. It's like yelling at a toddler for falling when they are learning to walk. It's not helpful, it's probably hurtful, and it's definitely mean, so just don't do it. You are a toddler learning to walk, and so am I. Be sweet to yourself. Praise yourself for trying. Celebrate every attempt, even if you just sat and thought about what you wanted for lunch. It's all good. Really, I promise.

Another tip that helped me when I was fighting with the entire idea of meditation was listening to the audiobook *Why Buddhism is True* by Robert Wright. This book describes a lot of the science behind meditation and was written by someone who struggled with it, as I did, in the beginning. Obviously, you could just as easily read the actual book, but in my mind, audiobooks are right up there with Netflix and the wheel in terms of great inventions. As parents, we spend so much time driving; might as well get a book in while you are dropping off or picking up or sitting in a carpool line, right?

Finally, like with a few of the other tips, having a meditation practice of her own is definitely something that will benefit your anxious child. And while you could try to simply tell your sweetie pie to go meditate and hope for the best, personally, I've always had more success with my (stubborn as a mule) anxious sweetie by doing it first. My little skeptical one is always more open when I practice whatever nonsense I'm preaching, and she's even more open when she can see that "Mom does seem a little less insane than usual. Perhaps there is something to that meditation stuff she keeps talking about."

Depending on your child's age, your sweetie may be totally willing to sit with you and do it together, and if so, there are actually some great books written especially for kids that might be helpful. *Sitting Still Like a Frog* by Eline Snel has some great tips and exercises for kids, and *I Am Peace* by Susan Verde, illustrated by Peter H. Reynolds (one of my very favorite illustrators of children's books. Go read *Ish*, right now), is a board book written directly to kids. But there are lots of great books for all ages out there. Older kids and teens might not be so willing to sit with you and might not even admit to you that they are doing it. Sometimes subtle suggestions like, "I got the Calm app on my phone. Want me to buy it for you too?" go over better with the too-cool-for-school teen in your house. I say, just like with your own meditation practice, do whatever works.

# CHAPTER 8:

# Coping Strategies— The Good, The Bad, and The Ugly

Coping strategies—goodness knows we need them. Everyone needs them. Even when you aren't dealing with an anxious child, you are always dealing with pressures, stress, deadlines, tough decisions, financial worries, health concerns, etc. Life isn't for the faint of heart, and we all figure out pretty early on those things that help us get through the tough times. In that sense, coping strategies are great. They have gotten us through some bad, hard, and tough stuff.

But here's the thing—and it's a tough thing, something we don't really like to admit to ourselves. There is a difference between taking care of yourself and escaping. This was a difficult chapter to write because this is a tricky topic, one that I have struggled with and continue to struggle with. There are no hard and fast rules when it comes to coping. Well, actually that's not true. There are some very clear good ways to cope and some very clear bad ways to cope. But between those, there is a whole world of options that are in between, kind of in a gray area. Some strategies are good some of the time and bad some of the time depending on lots of things like why you use them, when you use them, and how often you use them. As you think about how you tend to cope with hard times, maybe your coping strategy isn't the absolute best in the world, but it probably isn't the worst either. That's exactly what I would say about my own.

It's time to take a cold, hard look at a few of the most common coping strategies. As you do, I hope you will start to see where your strategies fall in that world of gray between really healthy coping and really unhealthy coping. My goal here is not that you will feel guilty or defensive or bad in any way about how you get through the tough times. What I do hope is that we can shine a light on things that most of us do without much thought at all. And in cases where your strategy isn't the most helpful or healthy, I hope I can help you determine a few other options you might try instead.

The point of this chapter, and the entire book really, is that when you're healthy, everyone around you will benefit. I wish I could come up with a really good rhyme to illustrate this point like "healthy mama, healthy llama" but that really doesn't work. "Heathy mother, healthy brother." No. "Healthy parent…" Um. Anyway, keep reading about coping strategies, and try to remember the better you are at this, the better it will be for you and for your anxious child and for everyone else around you.

And one more thing. Please remember what I said before. I'm not shooting for perfection and neither should you. What's really important about coping strategies and why I put all of this down in a chapter is this: you have to be really honest with yourself about what you are doing and why. People typically cope with stress and overwhelm in many different ways. I challenge you (and me) to really think about when you use each and, more importantly, why you use them.

What are the big buckets of coping strategies that exist? Typically, when we need to get through something, we do one or more of the following: we try to escape, we engage in compulsive behaviors, or we self-medicate. I can hear you now saying, "Jeesh, those sound like scary clinical or even criminal behaviors! I don't do any of those. I take bubble baths. I go for walks. What are you talking about, crazy lady?!!?"

Keep in mind that there are completely socially acceptable versions of each of those coping strategies that may or may not be healthy. Remember what I said; there's a whole lot of gray in the area of coping. Some strategies are healthy in some situations and not in others. And there are obviously some examples that just aren't healthy any way you look at them.

**Escaping**

Let's start with escaping. Escaping covers any sort of coping behavior that we do with the objective of simply escaping the situation either temporarily or permanently. Your preferred kind of escaping might be a real escape where you actually leave, or it could be a mental escape. Like all of these strategies, some versions of escaping are healthier than others. Taking a walk or a bubble bath are probably some of the most obvious acceptable examples of temporary escape. Jumping in your car and leaving your small kids unattended while you drive to Vegas to start a new life as a showgirl is, in my opinion, a less acceptable version of escape. And then there are a whole lot of options in the middle of those two.

A basic rule of thumb for evaluating an escape option you might use is simply this: if your idea to escape endangers you or anyone else, especially your kids, then it's unhealthy. If no one is hurt in any way by your escape, then it's probably OK as long as you don't overuse it. Here are a few more examples of ways people escape: reading a book, driving around, going to the mall, sitting in a beautiful place like a garden or park while your kids are with a sitter, or leaving your kids with your spouse so that you can do things with your friends. You get the picture.

I think the idea of escape is pretty easy to grasp. Compulsive behaviors, however, are a little more complex.

## Compulsive Behaviors

Using compulsive behaviors as a coping strategy sounds a bit scarier than escaping, doesn't it? But just like an escape, there is a wide range of compulsive behaviors, and some are more acceptable than others. Now, this is a very simplistic explanation of compulsive behaviors that many super-smart Freudians might take issue with, but for the purpose of you and me sitting here having coffee, the way we begin to develop compulsive behaviors is that we feel bad or uncomfortable (usually when we are quite young but not always). When we are feeling bad, we stumble across something that makes us feel better. And whatever it was that we stumbled across works so well that we just keep doing it. You might not realize it, but we all do this to different degrees and in different situations and to fix different problems. (Hello, nail biters, fidgeters, hair twisters. I'm talking to you.)

Compulsive behaviors become a problem when we can't stop doing the thing that made us feel better, which becomes a problem in and of itself. And (like every coping strategy) doing something compulsively can become a way of distracting us from feeling what we need to feel in order to get over what's making us feel bad in the first place. Compulsive behaviors are usually unconscious. We stop realizing we are even doing these things to cope. We just do them.

The most obvious example of compulsive behavior is overeating. It's easy to imagine someone experiencing stress or sadness finding that eating ice cream or chocolate cake (or *both*!) makes them feel better. We've all fallen prey to the "If a little makes me feel good, then a lot will make me feel even better" fallacy. And if you've never fallen for that line of thinking, take it from me; it isn't true, and a lot more never makes you feel better. In the case of overeating, the overreliance upon cake, or food in general, becomes a compulsion, something unconscious that happens without the person even realizing they are doing it. So the eating that made us feel better now becomes a health problem, and it distracts us from what we really need to do to feel better. The same thing can happen with undereating. A person loses a little weight and feels great. People notice. They feel better about themselves. They feel like they have control over one thing in a crazy uncontrollable world, and the desire to have more of that feeling can lead to eating less and less and eventually compulsively undereating. (Please note:

these are over-simplifications of complex problems simply to illustrate compulsive behaviors in general.)

The tricky thing about compulsive behaviors is that they aren't always as clear cut as overeating or starving yourself. As I said above, most people have some sort of compulsive behavior they use to distract themselves when they don't want to feel an unpleasant emotion. Some people compulsively exercise. Some people clean. Some jump into planning and doing in order not to feel—I was very guilty of that one when my mother passed away unexpectedly. And when a compulsive behavior is something that we think is good or virtuous, like exercising or cleaning, it is a little harder to criticize ourselves for doing it. Exercise isn't bad. Cleaning isn't bad. The issue is how often you do it and why. Anything that is done excessively to escape or avoid feeling what you're feeling can be a problem. And that goes for the benign examples of escaping I described above too. If you are obsessively reading novels while your life falls apart around you, that can be a problem.

Do you want to know what's the most common compulsive behavior I see every single day? Scrolling away on smartphones. Before you argue with me, take a second and really consider; do you ever pick up your phone in order to avoid feeling bored? Do you unconsciously scroll because at some point you learned that it helps you escape from uncomfortable feelings like boredom or, even worse, that awkward weirdness when you are around people you don't know? If your anxious child is old enough to have a phone, I guarantee this is a coping strategy your sweetie uses.

And that's what I mean by coping strategies often falling into gray areas. You probably don't need to seek treatment because you mindlessly scroll on your phone when you feel bored or uncomfortable. However, if I am being totally honest, and really, I never want to be anything but totally honest with you, I would argue that grabbing the phone or cleaning or running or planning or online shopping (hello my old friend, Amazon Prime) in order to escape feeling uncomfortable or sad or lonely is never a truly healthy thing.

### Self-Medication

Self-medicating has quite a lot in common with everything we just discussed regarding compulsive behaviors. It often starts innocently enough but when we realize that drinking alcohol, taking prescription pills, smoking cigarettes, etc. makes us feel better, we start doing that thing whenever we want to escape a bad feeling. When self-medicating turns into a full-blown addiction, it's pretty easy to agree that you've passed the gray area and are firmly in the unhealthy side of the equation.

The trickier thing about self-medicating is determining when socially accepted behaviors like having a glass of wine is really about avoiding your feelings. It easily starts to fall into the same category as scrolling on your phone or compulsive exercise or online shopping. My personal position is it's always good to check in with yourself and stay aware of how you are interacting with any mood-altering substance, even if it's a legal substance.

## How Can You Change Your Coping Strategies?

As you start to notice yourself escaping or doing something unconsciously to avoid how you're feeling, start asking yourself, "Is this the healthiest way to cope with whatever I am going through? Am I avoiding my feelings here?" If there's anything having an anxious child has taught me, it is that I need some good coping strategies. But it's also taught me that sometimes my go-to coping strategies weren't the healthiest, and I needed to figure out something new.

The bottom line of all of this is that there is a difference between self-care, showing yourself compassion and love, and soothing yourself, as all hurt animals need to do, versus doing something to distract or avoid feeling something you feel. And while everyone avoids their feelings to some degree or another, there is a point where it becomes truly problematic and unhealthy if you are always trying to avoid feeling what you feel. Our emotions are part of us. Always avoiding feeling any negative or uncomfortable feelings is a recipe for bigger problems down the road.

And of course, I can't go on without saying that if you know that you are struggling with any truly unhealthy compulsive, addictive, or self-medicating behaviors, you definitely need to seek assistance from someone trained to help you overcome this problem. It is impossible to be the kind of parent I know you want to be if you aren't healthy. Addictions and self-destructive compulsions are never healthy. However, there are so many avenues to help you get healthy. Don't beat yourself up, just find the help that works best for you.

If, however, you feel that you are generally using your coping strategies in healthy ways but you're like all of us and could stand to improve especially in terms of avoiding unpleasant feelings, well scootch over sister because I am right there with you.

### How I Fooled Myself into Believing My Coping Strategies Weren't So Bad

Here's just one example of a gray coping strategy from my life: I told you before that my brain creates all kinds of thoughts that aren't true, and I didn't realize it for years. Well, my brain also has come up with some pretty sneaky ways to self-medicate in order to manage my own sense of stress and overwhelm. My personal drug of choice is sugar, and if that sugar is delivered via some sort of starchy deliciousness, even better. So sometimes, my way of avoiding my feelings was to bake (and of course eat) chocolate chip cookies. I would always claim they were for my kids. I mean, that's what good moms do, right? They bake! Isn't baking chocolate chip cookies like stereotypical good momming? I share this example, one, because it is totally true and anyone who knows me knows it's true but also because it illustrates how sneaky these "coping strategies" can be. We can convince ourselves that we aren't really trying to avoid feeling uncomfortable feelings; we are just being good moms.

I also love Amazon, and I will admit I have been sucked into buying books for my kids, like a good mom, just to get that dopamine rush you get when you get a package. That's another sneaky example that I personally have used to avoid feeling bad feelings and to convince myself that I wasn't being avoidant. I was just being a good mom.

The trick in this is to really be "on to yourself." Really, and I mean really, look at those things you are doing and ask, why am I doing this? If you dig deep and notice that you might be using any of the coping strategies I describe above to avoid your feelings, then the first step is to simply notice. What do you do to cope? Any time you notice that you are using any of the strategies we discussed above, spend a bit of time trying to figure out why.

Try asking yourself "what am I feeling right now?" If you can't get really specific about your feelings, put them into the big buckets: mad, sad, glad, or afraid. Sometimes just acknowledging what you are feeling can bring some relief. Sometimes you need to sit with the feeling for a little while. Remember all of those times that you cried your eyes out when you were young (or maybe not so young or maybe last week)? Did you feel better when you were done? That's a common example of feeling what you feel no matter how unpleasant and sitting with it until it passes. If, however, you find that the feeling isn't passing, there are a couple more things you can do.

When we find ourselves stuck in bad feelings, that's a good time to jump back over to Chapter 4 and look at those thoughts that are creating the bad feelings. Are you making something mean something else that's much worse? Is it true?

## When Questioning Your Thoughts Still Isn't Enough

Sometimes in order to get to the heart of why you are feeling bad feelings, you need to dig even deeper than you did in Chapter 4. Sometimes you need to really look at the scared, wounded parts of yourself. Sometimes you need to reconnect with the part of yourself that originally felt bad and learned to overeat or compulsively plan or shop online or step outside for a cigarette in order to feel better. We all have these. Psychologists often refer to it as "your inner child." When you want to shift to healthier coping methods, you might first need to become friends with your inner child or the part of you that adopted that unhealthy coping method in the first place.

The term self-care is often misunderstood. People assume it just means bubble baths, but it's really about asking your inner child what it wants and giving it to him or her. Do you know what most inner children crave? Attention. Try writing in a journal as your inner child. Or try role-playing and ask what would make your inner child feel better. You can free write or answer out loud. Instead of eating chocolate chip cookies, my inner child really loves watching a movie at a movie theater.

The way you make friends with your inner child is to first become still and present enough to feel what it wants and then just be really nice to yourself. Treat yourself like you would treat your own sweet child if they had had a bad day. Speak kindly to yourself. Take it easy. Offer yourself the kinds of things you would offer a sick child: a nap, a warm bath, a story (i.e. a movie or a good book). While I am often skeptical of the big three coping strategies I list above—escaping, compulsive behaviors, and self-medicating—because I realize they tend to happen when we are avoiding our feelings, I am always a fan of good old-fashioned self-care and compassion. Just showing compassion to yourself and being kind to yourself can fix a lot of stubborn problems.

If you're feeling a little uncomfortable with the whole idea of an inner child and trying to communicate with it, I understand. It does feel a little odd at first. Sometimes this is easier when you work with a therapist who can guide you. If you aren't quite ready for that option, try the writing or role playing and simply notice those little things that make you and your inner child happy. Try to incorporate more of them into your day-to-day life. Do you like reading but never make time for it? Read. Like dancing? Dance around your house to music you love. There are lots of ways to practice self-care and they don't have to be big. The secret is to notice, and the bigger secret is to appreciate and really allow yourself to feel grateful for those things that make you happy. I love the smell of grapefruit essential oil. I add it to my lotion and try to take a moment to acknowledge the smell and how much I like it each time I use it. Simple, easy, and an act of self-care every time I do it.

And don't discount all of the tools you've learned up until this point. They are all examples of self-care. Identifying your feelings, questioning your thoughts, quieting your mind, repeating your mantra, meditation, they are all great ways to practice self-care with the added benefits of not encouraging you to avoid your feelings. In fact, using the tools to quiet your mind and feel into your gut is a great way to figure out what you really crave. My go-to, chocolate chip cookies, may not actually be what your soul is looking for, but you must become still and quiet to realize that.

So that's a quick overview of coping strategies and how you and I can try to improve on our go-to methods of escaping our feelings. But all of this talk of chocolate chip cookies has me thinking that it's time for another recipe. I would share my secret chocolate chip cookie recipe, but it turns out, I do not have a secret recipe. The world's best chocolate chip cookie recipe is already printed on the back of every package of Tollhouse chocolate chips. Don't waste time on others. Trust me. I've tried a lot (see above), and you just can't beat that one.

However, if you are looking for dinner before your cookies (no judgment if cookies are dinner), here are recipes for another two meals you can make with one protein.

**Peachy Grilled Pork Tenderloin and Pork Lo Mein**

*Peachy Grilled Pork Tenderloin*
*Ingredients:*

- 2 decent sized pork tenderloins (you need enough to have leftovers)
- 3/4 cup firmly packed Brown sugar
- 1/4 cup Kosher salt
- 2 cups boiling water

- 3 cups ice cubes
- 1/2 cup Dijon mustard
- 1/2 cup peach preserves
- fresh rosemary
- side dish(es) of your choice

I got this Peachy Pork Tenderloin recipe from *Family Fun* magazine, and it was a hit with everyone in my family, which never happens. So, obviously, when it was relatively easy to make and everyone ate it, it was a keeper. It does require marinating/brining ahead of time, but throw it in the fridge the morning or even the night before you want to eat it, and when you're ready to cook dinner, it won't take any time at all to get it on the table. Or you can cut the brining time down to thirty minutes if you're in a rush.

Mix your salt and sugar in a large glass storage container big enough to hold both tenderloins and the water and ice. Add the boiling water and stir until the salt and sugar are mostly dissolved. Add your ice cubes (full disclosure, I don't measure the ice cubes. I add a few "scoops" using the scoop that came with my ice maker and call it good). When your brine is cool, add the pork tenderloins. Cover and refrigerate either overnight, all day, or for at least thirty minutes. (I've also made the brine in a big glass bowl and poured it over the tenderloins in a big 2-gallon zip-lock bag. Whatever you've got will work.)

When you are ready to cook, preheat your grill. Mix a ½ cup of mustard and a ½ cup of peach preserves in a bowl, then add chopped rosemary to taste (I use about 1 tablespoon). Take half of this sauce and put it in another small bowl. You are going to use one of these bowls of sauce to baste on the pork in the last five minutes of cooking and will serve the other bowl with the pork.

Remove the pork from the brine. The recipe says you should rinse it thoroughly. However, I am a little heebed out by handling and rinsing raw meat in my sink, so I always skip that step, and it's never seemed to matter. It's up to you. Cook them on the grill for around twenty minutes, turning them every five minutes or so. In the last five minutes of cooking, from one of the bowls, baste ½ of the sauce you created. You want the tenderloins to reach 145 degrees (63 degrees Celsius if you are outside of the US), so pull out that meat thermometer. When they are cooked and basted, remove them from heat and let them rest tented with foil for five minutes before cutting. Serve with the reserved peach/mustard sauce and the sides of your choice.

I hope everyone in your family loves the tenderloin. But I hope they don't love it so much that you don't have any left because you need the leftovers for dinner number two.

### *Lo Mein with Pork*
### *Ingredients:*

- Leftover pork cut into bite-sized pieces
- Lo Mein noodles or Udon or any spaghetti-like noodles, including regular old spaghetti. This recipe calls for 3/4 pound, but I have absolutely no idea how to measure 3/4 pound of noodles, so I just prepare the same amount I would prepare with any pasta meal for my family.
- Vegetable oil (I use Canola)
- Mushrooms (I use two packages of pre-sliced mushrooms, but you can use less or even omit them if your family doesn't like mushrooms)
- 1/2 to a whole red or yellow bell pepper sliced into very thin slices
- Snow peas sliced into thin slices (I grab a couple of handfuls if they are for sale in bulk, or I just use a couple of handfuls out of the package if in a package)
- Garlic to taste. This Recipe calls for 9 cloves of minced garlic. I am not a big fan of mincing garlic, so I buy the pre-minced in the jar and use a big whopping tablespoon)
- 1/2 teaspoon—1 tablespoon grated ginger (I use the kind in the jar, but you can certainly use fresh. My kids don't love lots of ginger, so

I tend to use less but if you are a ginger-loving family, go nuts.)
- Soy sauce or liquid aminos or coconut aminos—whatever you've got. You'll need a healthy amount, probably 4+ tablespoons.
- 1 tablespoon or close to of toasted sesame oil

This Lo Mein recipe is an adaptation of a Martha Stewart recipe. My family likes their Lo Mein a bit sweeter than Martha's version, so I added a few more tablespoons of the same peach preserves I used in the glaze and sauce last night. That may sound weird, but I promise you don't taste the peaches, and your kids will eat it.

### *Instructions*

Cook your noodles according to the package directions then drain them.

In a large skillet or wok, heat a few teaspoons of oil over medium-high heat. Add garlic and ginger and saute for a minute being careful not to burn your garlic. Add the mushrooms and cook until they soften and release their juices. The recipe says four minutes, but it always seems to take at least twice that long. Once your mushrooms seem really soft and cooked, add bell pepper strips and sauté until crisp-tender for around four minutes. Add snow peas and cook until crisp and bright green for around two minutes.

Now dump the noodles into the skillet. I hope you knew I was serious when I said a large skillet. Add in your leftover pork cut into strips or bite-sized pieces. Squirt enough soy sauce over the noodles to cover them (recipe says 3 tablespoons, but I never measure), and add a couple of spoonfuls of the peach preserves. Stir for a few minutes until the preserves sort of melt into the rest of the sauce and the pork heats through. Remove from heat. Drizzle with sesame oil before serving.

Easy peasy, lemon squeezy, and that's another two dinners in one. You're welcome!

# CHAPTER 9:

# Who's in the Circle?
# Create a Support System that
# Really Supports

So as I sat down to write a chapter about support systems, I found myself procrastinating by scrolling through my Facebook feed. I said I was going to be honest with you, and that's the honest truth. I was messing around, wasting time on Facebook instead of writing, and lo and behold, what do I see? A sweet and obviously terrified mom of a kindergartner had posted in a local "mommy" FB group asking for advice. In this group of approximately 1,300 moms, she shared her story that her child is having serious anxiety and refusing to go to school. Of course, I then took a moment to scroll through the many responses. People were kind. People were sympathetic. People really wanted to help—but in my opinion, many of them were totally making things worse.

This Facebook interaction was, first and foremost, a little smack upside my head from God (The universe, Source, you remember the drill. I don't care what you call him). That sweet kindergarten mom illustrated perfectly why we need support and why we need to be careful about how and where we get that support.

Parenting is hard. Parenting an anxious child is definitely hard. For parents, the universal "hardness" of parenting is what bonds us. It's what we have in common with that mom who may not even speak English but can express empathy when we are carrying a screaming toddler out of the grocery store. With just a look, another parent can let us know, "Yep, I've been there too. I feel you."

But just like anything that's hard—like sports or the Miss America Pageant—parenting can also bring out the worst in us. Parents judge each other. Parents can be super competitive. Parents tell you things like "My perfect three-year-old prodigy plays Mozart on the violin, speaks fluent Russian, and just got her early acceptance letter from Harvard" before asking, "Oh, but how are you doing with that social skills training class? Is it helping your sweetie pie?" Sometimes, other parents are mean. Sometimes, other parents are clueless. Often, we aren't even sure which.

It's because it's so tough that we need support. Parenting is not something to try to tackle on your own. You might not like the saying "It takes a village" any more than I like "Put on your own oxygen mask first," but they are both true, and in this chapter, I want to talk about that village. Who should (and should not) be in it? How do you create it? And how you can avoid the inevitable debacle of asking a thousand moms for advice on Facebook.

## The Circle

So, let's start at the beginning. In my family, my siblings and I use the phrase "in the circle" to describe the people we trust and are closest to. I have no idea where that saying came from. Maybe everyone says it? For example, we might say something like, "Well, William has always had a big circle," meaning he just likes everyone. Or we might say, "You know how Bill is. He is sweet and loving, but once you're out of the circle, you are out for good." I share this weird little anecdote about my family because I think "the circle" is a great way to talk about our support systems.

We all have lots of people in our lives, and I would never advocate for getting rid of anyone you want to keep. However, the way I recommend looking at your support system is "Are they in the circle or not?" You can love some friends and family members while keeping them out of the circle if they don't meet the criteria for being a member of your support team. It's totally OK. I give you permission. You get to decide who's in the circle and who's out.

So with that said, we're going to need some basic criteria to determine who's in the circle and who's not. I could come up with a nice list of objective criteria that includes all kinds of fancy things like degrees, travel and life experiences, marital status, etc. But, at the end of the day, I really don't think those things do such a great job of sorting who should get in. However, what will really come in handy in determining who's in and who's out is all of the time you've spent in the previous chapters figuring out how to get calm and listen to your gut and ask yourself what you are feeling.

To start, here are a few criteria I use to determine who's in my parent support circle:

- People who generally refrain from judgment, i.e., non-judgey types
- People who have been there or are there now
- People who seem to get it even if they haven't actually been there
- People who just love me and my kid no matter what

That's not a long list, but it really sums up who gets in. But what did I mean by the tools we learned in the previous chapters are going to come in handy? Well, unfortunately for us all, people don't walk around wearing t-shirts that say "I judge you." While the list above describes who gets to be in my circle, just having the list isn't the only tool I need to determine who's in and who's out. I meet new people all of the time. It usually takes a while to really get to know people or to figure out if they meet the criteria. Sometimes I'm just not sure. What do I do then?

When I am in doubt, I trust my instincts. I trust my gut. I trust my intuition. And do you know how I know what my gut and intuition are saying?? You guessed it. I use all of the tools we've covered in the previous chapters. When I get a bad feeling about someone, I try to quiet my mind and just feel it. I try to identify the bad feeling (mad, sad, afraid) and then identify the thought that is causing the feeling. I question my thoughts. I ask myself, "Is it true?" I try to get really clear on where that bad feeling is coming from.

Sometimes, when I dig deep, I realize my bad feelings have nothing to do with the other person and everything to do with me. Sometimes, when I feel insecure or embarrassed, I make it about the other person. I try to blame other people for my feelings. I tell myself, "I feel this way because they are so judgey." But when I use the tools, I realize my feelings are the result of thoughts that aren't even true. Sometimes, I felt embarrassed because of what I was making something mean. The other person wasn't really judging me at all.

However, there are other times when my intuition is very clear and says, "This person just isn't your cup of tea." And when I ask myself if that's true, I get a resounding yes. And you know what? When my intuition says that, I've learned to listen. I can't tell you how many times I have found myself in an uncomfortable situation with someone who I knew was not my cup of tea, but I ignored it or second-guessed myself or tried to talk myself out of thinking that by making myself feel guilty. I've let people into the circle despite clear messages from my gut, and it never went well.

Once I gave myself permission to keep people out of my circle, I found myself in uncomfortable positions much less frequently. Keeping someone out of your circle doesn't mean you hate them or that you are enemies or that you'll never socialize or be friendly. That's just something my silly brain tried to make it mean. Did you notice the words I used above? I just said, "They aren't my cup of tea." I didn't say, "They are terrible human beings and I hope they die" because that would be a little nutty. But saying someone isn't your cup of tea doesn't have to mean anything about them. I'm not everyone's cup of tea, either. That's just how the world works and it's totally OK.

So, if you are like me and you find yourself feeling a little guilty when you want to exclude someone from your circle, try my phrase above. "They just aren't my cup of tea." A short list of people who will never be my cup of tea includes:

- Anyone who feels the need to point out my screwups to me or to other people in a mean-spirited way. I'm all about laughing at my screwups, however.
- Anyone who I consistently feel terrible after interacting with. That's a huge hint from my intuition that I ignore at my own peril.
- Anyone who seems to look for negative things in me or in others to make themselves look or feel better about themselves.
- Anyone who engages in schadenfreude—taking pleasure in someone else's misfortune.
- Anyone who makes everything into a catastrophe.
- Anyone who always assumes the absolute worst about everything.
- Anyone who pushes me too hard to take their advice even when it's clear I'm not comfortable doing what they are telling me to do.

That list sums up what I saw in the Facebook comments I mentioned at the beginning of this chapter. There were probably elements of all of them, but I especially saw examples of the last two. There were people, regular people not psychiatrists, psychologists, or medical doctors, throwing out diagnoses. People were sure that something traumatic had happened to the kindergartner. People had all sorts of advice like go to the school, talk to the principal and the teacher, and sit and observe. And all I could think of as I read all of the comments (I just popped back over to FB, and as of this minute there are 157 comments on that post) was how I felt when my child started kindergarten. It was new and scary enough without 157 people telling me my child had probably been traumatized in some way and I should be up at that school demanding action. Please keep in mind, she posted on the fifth day of school. I'm not saying that the commenters were right or wrong. What I am saying is that I'm not sure that the good—trying to be helpful and supportive, and I believe everyone who commented actually meant well—outweighed the bad—freaking a mother out and filling her head with possibilities she hadn't even considered—in this interaction.

The point of having a circle isn't to exclude or to be cliquish or to live out your mean girl fantasies from high school. It's just about the same thing that every tip in this book has been about: how to get and keep yourself as healthy as you can be so that you are able to be the parent you want to be. Try to think of questioning your thoughts and trusting your intuition and meditating, and creating a healthy circle as the equivalent of taking your mom vitamins.

The biggest challenge I face and see other moms face in creating the perfect circle tends to be guilt. We feel guilty not inviting Jane to coffee even though Jane always makes us feel like the worst mother on the planet. I've said this a couple of times in this chapter, but I am going to say it again because most of us need to hear it over and over and over again. You have permission to exclude people from your circle. You will figure out over time how to do it and what it means, but you are allowed to do it whenever your intuition gives you a strong message that that's what you need to do.

In my case, I have lots of friends but only a very small number of friends who I turn to for advice about my kids. The circle with whom I share details about my children's struggles tends to be small, and it includes that list I shared above. I talk to people who won't judge me, people who are or have been there too, and especially those amazing few who I know love me no matter how badly I screwed up.

If you're reading this, there is a decent chance that you have lost your temper with your child and then realized that the reason your child was misbehaving or not cooperating was that your sweetie was overwhelmed by anxiety and was possibly in the middle of a panic attack. I've done it. And realizing what I had done was one of the worst feelings I've experienced as a mom. Do you know what helped me when I was doubled over with shame? Having another mom, a great mom, tell me she had done the same. I wasn't alone. I wasn't the worst mom ever. And my sweetie pie would probably be OK, just like my friend's child was OK.

Having the right circle can save you. It certainly has saved me on many occasions. Because I think it's so important, here is one more list. These are people I recommend being included in anyone's circle, especially if your child struggles with anxiety.

- Family members who love you and your child without exception
- Friends who know you well enough to give you the benefit of the doubt and assume you're doing your best
- Parents in a similar situation with whom you can vent
- Professionals (e.g. a great pediatrician, your child's counselor, teachers, school staff, etc.) who listen and make you feel heard and supported.
- Someone (a friend, a counselor, therapist, or coach) whose main focus is just you—not your child, your marriage, or your job—just you.

If you are in a situation where you are having a hard time finding your circle, the best thing you can do is to go out into the real world and do something you want to do anyway. You might have expected me to say join a mom's group, but actually, I would only recommend that if you want to join a mom's group. If you'd rather take tap dancing lessons (and girl, me too!!), then you should do that. Or a cooking class. Or a professional women's organization. Or a running club. Do something you love doing with other people, and you are more likely to meet "your people." I could write an entire chapter or probably even a book on how much more interesting, fun, and attractive you are when you are doing something you love instead of doing something you think you are supposed to do or that you believe might help you meet people.

It's like the field of dreams. If you just do you, they will come.

# CHAPTER 10:

# Putting It All Together

Last night was parent night at my son's school. Here's another true confession for you: I hate parent night. I always have. It always feels like the last thing I want to do when it comes around. Am I right? However, my son is a junior in high school as I write this, so the realization that I only have one more parent night for him after this one makes me tear up a little. Every "only one more" for him makes me tear up. It's starting to become a thing. He says, "Please, don't start crying, Mom," on a regular basis.

But anyway, back to parent night. One of the surprising high points of parent night for me was Algebra II. Surprising because algebra was probably my least favorite class in high school, closely followed by chemistry. However, his teacher seemed fun and enthusiastic, which I love, and she entertained us with a list of reasons why the boys (my son goes to an all-boys school. It's a "thing" where I live in Louisiana) should do their homework. Her analogy was that she can watch the Saints play football all season, but she still won't be able to play football.

Her analogy made me think of this terrible habit I have of purchasing some sort of videotape or DVD or streaming access to an exercise program every ten years or so. Each time I do it, I am totally convinced I really will use it. And I never do. That's why it only happens every ten years. That's how long it takes me to forget the last wasted purchase.

I don't know if you are sensing a theme here, but I'll make it easy for you. Nothing works if you don't do it. You don't learn algebra by watching the teacher do problems. You don't become a great quarterback by watching the Saints. You don't get buns of steel just by purchasing a DVD. And you certainly aren't going to manage your child's anxiety any better by just reading this book.

I wish it were that easy. I really do. You have no idea how awesome my body would be right now if it worked that way. You've now read each of the tips and techniques, but reading just isn't enough. The trick (to everything in life really) is, as Nike says, to just do it.

Will it be easy? Probably not. Again, I wish I could say yes, but the pesky logic center of my brain says if it were easy, you would already be doing it. However, like most hard things (e.g. training to run a marathon, childbirth, finishing school, or growing out your bangs), it will be totally worth it. I can say that without any doubt because of my own experience and knowing what using these techniques has done for me.

So now that that's out of the way, here are some techniques on how to put them all together and use them in real life (IRL).

### So Let's Review

The very first thing covered in this book was the concept that anxiety is actually a normal human phenomenon. You learned why anxious, fearful, and nervous feelings and thoughts are simply part of our evolutionary history and how in the not so distant past; being super fearful was actually something that helped our ancestors stay alive.

The reason I started with the argument that anxiety is a normal part of being human was because "This isn't normal" and "My child isn't normal" are some very common painful thoughts that we parents of anxious children tend to struggle with. I wanted to start by giving you some evidence to refute that thought. Unfortunately for us, when we are dealing with really well-established, painful thoughts, the evidence isn't always enough to make us feel better.

Therefore, the next concept discussed was what you can do to get some relief from those sticky painful thoughts. You learned the importance of feeling our feelings and first noticing then learning to question those recurrent painful thoughts. In order to really get to the heart of those sticky persistent thoughts, I introduced the "What am I making this mean?" or the "So?" technique to dig deeper and deeper until you are really clear on what is at the heart of your pain. And once the root thought is identified, it may have been something like "I can't handle this," or "I'm failing as a mother," or "My child will never have friends." You learned to ask yourself, "Is it true?" and "Can I absolutely know that it's true?"

The act of questioning whether your painful thoughts are true and eventually seeing that they may not be true can be a game-changer. First, it can change you as a parent. It can start to take away the underlying fear, pain, and anxiety you are experiencing as you parent your anxious child. And secondly, as you change, you can show and teach your child how to use the same technique to help them change.

The two fundamental concepts that jumped out from the discussion are: anxiety is a normal thing, and your thoughts aren't always true. These ideas were your starting point because they gave you some key ideas that you will continue to use as you tackle a few of the more tangible, everyday problems parents of anxious kids face.

For example, being judged by friends, family, and even strangers is an all too common experience among parents of anxious kids, and feeling your feelings and questioning your thoughts are super helpful techniques for dealing with judgment. In fact, that's where I always start when I am feeling judged by anyone else. I ask myself what I am feeling and then dig into what I am thinking that's creating that feeling. When I get to the heart of the matter, I ask myself if my thought is true, and if it isn't, I can let it go and begin to feel better.

However, sometimes you believe the judgment is true. What do you do when someone is judging you, and you agree with them? In that case, you have to answer a few additional questions: is the judgment related to something you can control? If no, turn it over to a higher power, and let it go. If it is something you can control, you then must ask yourself if you care enough to do anything about it? If the answer is no, give it to a higher power, and let it go. If, however, you can control it and you care enough to do something about it, do something or find support to help and give it to a higher power, and let it go.

Handling advice can be similar to handling judgment because we often make it mean something, and then we need to revisit the tools above to determine what we are thinking and if that thought is even true. But in addition to making advice mean something, there's also the issue with information overload. Parents often get so much advice from so many sources we can't process much less act on it all. When that happens, the first step I take is to breathe. However, if I am feeling too overwhelmed even to breathe, I add a mantra like "I am determined to see this with love." And once I've calmed my freaking-out, overactive brain down, I tune into my gut and intuition to determine which advice feels right for me and my child. I have learned to give myself permission to try things and to give up when it just isn't working.

But there's another technique that has proven invaluable to calming my freaking out, overactive brain, and that's meditation. Meditation can be harder than it seems, and one thing that makes it harder is starting with expectations of what is supposed to happen or how it's supposed to work. To help learn this tool that can be so helpful to me and my anxious child, I first had to "Lighten up, Francis," and just try it. I also had to accept the fact that beating myself up for not being a good meditator is completely counterproductive. Instead, I simply tried many different types of meditation. The secret to becoming a meditator is to relax and use the type of meditation that seems to work for you and to keep at it even when you feel like you aren't "doing it right."

Even with all of these tips and techniques, we all find ourselves having bad days (and weeks and sometimes even months). When that happens, we need ways to help us cope. The typical ways people cope are by escaping, turning to compulsive behaviors, and self-medicating. And while there are socially acceptable examples of all of these, at the end of the day, I've learned that the best way to cope is to allow myself to feel my discomfort. Once I've felt my feelings, no matter how unpleasant, the next step is to determine what would comfort the part of me that is sad, tired, or hurting? Once I get in touch with the part of me that is trying to escape or use compulsive behaviors or self-medicate, I can determine what I really need to feel better in a healthy way. The most important thing I've learned about coping is that being kind to yourself and showing yourself compassion are never bad ways to cope.

Parenting is tough with or without the added complication of anxiety. In addition to needing ways to cope, you also need a circle of special, trusted people to help you along this parenting journey. Getting calm and feeling into your gut can be extremely helpful tools in determining who should be in and who should be out of your circle. A key thing to remember as you are forming and maintaining your circle is that you have permission to decide. You don't have to feel guilty or feel like you are being mean. It's OK to decide when someone just isn't your cup of tea.

So that's everything in a really small nutshell. As I said at the beginning, it won't work if you don't do it. I want to leave you with a simple checklist with the hope that boiling it all down to the simplest level will make you more likely to stick with it.

- Feel your feelings
- Question your thoughts
- Calm down
- Ask your gut and intuition what to do to make yourself feel better
- Do what your gut and intuition tell you
- Accept support from the right people (the circle)
- Repeat, repeat, repeat

Make a copy of this, put it in places where you can grab it, and look at it whenever you find yourself struggling.

You might need to revisit the tools and reread the chapters, especially if you find yourself struggling with one specific area. You may want to dig deeper with additional resources if necessary to really make it click. If you find yourself struggling with any one topic, there are books, websites, apps, etc. that can help. And of course, you can find me online, and I would love to hear from you.

It won't be easy, but as I said, nothing worthwhile ever is. We aren't going for perfection, just forward progress. And like so many other concepts we've discussed, there's science to back me up on this. Progress begets more progress. It's called momentum. Starting is hard. Continuing is easier. Even easier if you don't have unrealistic goals or expectations. Lighten up, Francis, and try it. That's all you have to do.

# CHAPTER 11:

# The Top Three Ways
# I Screwed Up

Remember those analogies I started the last chapter with? You don't learn how to do algebra by watching the teacher. You don't get a bikini body by buying videos. The point was that you have to do it. But there's actually a part B to the analogy. Just because you do your Algebra homework, that's not a guarantee that you will always get a 100 on the test.

As I write this, my children are finishing their third week of a new school year. I had been bracing myself because I know how anxiety works. It's an opportunistic condition. It often feels to me as if it's lying in wait. When my daughter is tired, not eating well (and in this case, literally starving herself because she's convinced she needs to lose weight before homecoming, sigh...) and generally using all of her reserve energy to make it through school, homework, and the inevitable social drama, anxiety sees the opportunity and steps in. That's basically what happened this week.

When things are going well, it's so easy to feel smug, as if I've completely mastered the tools and am on top of everything. However, when things aren't going so smoothly, when you sense your child might be spiraling downward and you can never be sure how far down this particular spiral your sweetie might go, that's when just doing it gets hard. And that's when just doing it is more important than ever. I cannot be the mom I want to be without feeling my feelings, meditating, questioning my thoughts, using healthy coping strategies, and leaning on the right people for support. It is precisely when I feel too busy or stressed to do those things that I need to do them most of all.

As I've said before, just doing it is the biggest obstacle I've faced and have seen other parents face when trying to make this program work for them. However, I have to come clean with you and admit that there are a few other things I've done wrong and have seen other people do wrong. So, before we check the boxes and feel a false sense of confidence that we've gotten through all of the tips together and we've got this, it probably makes sense to spend just a few pages talking about some of those mistakes so that maybe you can learn with a little less pain than I did.

## One Right Way to Do It and One Definition of Success

We might as well start with a big mistake that I made before my kids were even born. When I was pregnant, I felt so ill-equipped. I worried that I had no idea what I was going to do with this baby when it arrived. I read pregnancy and baby care books like it was my job. And somehow, as I obsessively prepared, I got this crazy idea in my head. I started to believe that there was one right way to parent. And later as my children grew and I began to see who they were, I believed that there was one right way to help an anxious child. I had a vision of success and anything other than that one very specific vision was not success.

Let me tell you, this idea that there's only one way to do something and only one successful outcome is a heavy weight to carry around. When I was dragging around this big fat idea of how I was "supposed" to be and how my kids were "supposed" to be and the way our lives were "supposed" to be, it was completely impossible for me to see that the life I actually had was pretty darn good.

And based on living my life and on my work as a coach, I'd say this idea that there's only one definition of success is pretty common. I mean for many of us, the entire Christmas season is a big fat obsession with one specific vision that often causes us to miss out on the happy kids that are in front of us.

I've had several clients struggle with holding on so tightly to one idea of success that they couldn't see the success in front of them. I once worked with a mother who spent months and months of our coaching sessions focused on the fact that her sweetie pie hadn't been accepted into a particular school. During those months, her sweetie pie was attending another school, making new friends, making good grades, and generally doing well. However, because my client had created one specific vision for her sweetie's future, anything else seemed to be wrong and a failure.

Clinging too tightly to one vision of success or one right way to do things is a common mistake and one I hope you can avoid more easily than I did. The tools in this book are the same tools that helped me tackle this issue. Breathing, getting out of my head, and appreciating what was happening right here and now were key to breaking my habit of missing good things that didn't meet my definition of success. Meditating on a regular basis helped me calm down enough to relax and see the good all around me as well.

**Boot Camp Parenting**

Unfortunately, however, redefining success wasn't the only thing I had to learn. After reading about my trials with meditation and trying to achieve nirvana—this probably won't come as a surprise at all—but another of my biggest mistakes was treating parenting like boot camp. I was willing to make it burn. It was all or nothing. I was going to white-knuckle it through this parenting gig all while smiling through my gritted teeth.

I had this basic idea that it had to be hard. If it wasn't hard, if I wasn't struggling all of the time, that meant I wasn't trying hard enough. My idea of being a good parent really was like boot camp, and I mean the one in *An Officer and a Gentleman* where they were doing pushups and sit-ups and running in the rain. Just like that version of boot camp, there was a loud mean angry drill sergeant in my head who was yelling day and night about all of the things I had done wrong and all of the ways I screwed up and all of the things everyone else thought about me.

The drill sergeant wasn't really trying to be mean. He only wanted to make me better. That voice was pointing out all of my mistakes and failures so I could improve. But over time, it became clear to me that the yelling and belittling and being mean to make me better just didn't work. I mean it really, *really* didn't work. In fact, it was the exact opposite of what did work.

It wasn't until I was able to treat myself with kindness and compassion that I was able to make any progress at all. But just like I am completely convinced the God Box and meditating works, I am also completely convinced that being nice to myself worked.

To illustrate my point, I'll give you one example: my life and my kids' lives and everyone else's lives started to improve when I learned how to replace the drill sergeant in my head with a voice that was nice to me. Instead of focusing on every mistake I made or reliving every bad interaction I had with my child, I started focusing on the ways I got it right, no matter how small, and that's when things started to get better for all of us. Remember healthy mama, healthy llama? I know. It's still a terrible slogan, but I'm just saying that everyone got better when I got better. It didn't happen overnight, and I am definitely not saying I don't still screw up all of the time or that the drill sergeant doesn't still show up because she does. But little by little, I make changes. And little by little, I see improvements for everyone, not just me.

This is a long-term and slow process. I started very small. On the worst days, maybe all I did was notice the drill sergeant voice and take a few breaths to get it out of my head. But that in itself was something. When I started focusing on that something that went well or that I did right, I was able to start building momentum for more somethings. Simply using the tools was progress. I didn't have to achieve anything with the tools. Just doing it was all I shot for. When I stopped and breathed, it was progress. When I meditated, it was progress. When I trusted my intuition and chose the advice to follow or ignore, it was progress. I celebrated that I did it. It didn't matter if the rest of the day went downhill. I celebrated the good, and by doing so, I created more good.

**If You Screw Up, Just Quit**

The white-knuckled drill sergeant approach to parenting is very related to yet another way that I was often tempted to mess up in my journey to becoming the best mom I can be at a given time. When I was convinced that I could treat parenting like boot camp and just yell and belittle myself into submission, I also thought that when I screwed up, I probably should just quit trying. Maybe I didn't meditate for a week or two or I spent days worrying about something another parent had said without bothering to dig into what I was making it mean or if it was even true. It wasn't great when I didn't use the tools because as I said, none of this stuff works unless you do it. But to make things worse, when I realized that I wasn't using the tools, a little part of me would throw up my hands and say, "See? You aren't doing it right. You should just give up."

And when that voice told me to give up, I relied on that other voice, the one that was nice to me, to step in. The nice voice reminded me that I don't have to be perfect. It said I was doing great. The nice voice was so excited that I noticed I hadn't been meditating and celebrated that as progress. It said things like, "A year ago, you didn't meditate at all. Look at you! Now you notice when you aren't doing it! Isn't that awesome? Hooray for you!!"

## What Does Work?

The thing that makes me tear up a little as I write this (I told you it was becoming a thing) is that when I started really listening to that nice voice, when I started encouraging myself and noticing the good things and celebrating progress not perfection, I started using that same nice voice with my kids more and more. I hate to admit that when the drill sergeant was the lead voice in my head, it was also the lead voice in the way I talked to my family. Letting the nice voice have a bigger role changed everything! It changed the way I felt inside. It changed the way I talked to my kids. It changed our relationship. It made our lives easier—not perfect, by any standard, but easier and happier and better.

I don't know if you noticed the words I used above to describe what I've been doing. I said, "I am on a journey to becoming the best mom I can be at a given time." I've said I'm not trying to be perfect about a million times, but I like this description of what I am trying to do quite a lot. I like it because when I say it, it doesn't freak me out or make me feel bad. It doesn't let me off the hook either. I am trying, but I am also acknowledging that all I can do is the best I can do in this moment. Sometimes I screw up. Sometimes, I'm tired, and I lose my temper. It may not be perfect, but it was my best in that moment, and I get to try to do better next time. I also can apologize when I screw up.

Apologizing is huge. Kids really need to see us acknowledge that we screwed up, that we know it, and that we are sorry. It helps them see that everybody screws up sometimes and the world doesn't end. People can even own up to their mistakes and keep going. Super important lesson for our anxious babies who are afraid to try things because they don't want to screw up. We can show them it happens. We can show them what to do when it does. We can show them that it will be OK because that's another thing my nice voice says to me, and I believe it. My nice voice is a Bob Marley fan. My nice voice sings sometimes. She loves "Three Little Birds" by Bob Marley and the Wailers.

So that brings me full circle back to the beginning of the chapter. I started by telling you that it was the third week of school and anxiety was starting to rear its ugly head and torment my sweetie pie. So how am I coping right now as I am writing this, as things aren't going perfectly and I am worried about my own child's anxiety flaring out of control?

I'm starting by noticing how I am feeling and just feeling it. It makes me scared, so I am being kind to myself. I'm reminding myself I don't have to be perfect. My sweetie doesn't have to be perfect. Our lives don't have to be perfect. I'm focused on kindness and self-compassion. I'm definitely seeing the progress and reminding myself of how far we both have come.

A few years ago, we both might be spiraling out of control. But right now, we're focused on taking care of ourselves and using the tools we've found that work for us.

I'm filled with gratefulness for where we are. It definitely isn't the vision of success I had when my kids were babies, but it feels pretty darn good right now. I'm celebrating that good. I'm reminding myself that I wasn't trying to be perfect and that I don't ever have to be perfect. I'm lightening up, Francis. And right now, in this moment, I'm doing OK. And I'm singing a little Bob Marley tune called "Three Little Birds." Go look it up on YouTube. Sing along with me.

CHAPTER 12:

# You Got This—Seriously, You Do!

You did it. You read this whole book! Look at you! You are a rock star!!

Hey, don't even think about arguing with me here. My nice voice has some really important things to say to you, and your drill sergeant needs to calm down and hear me.

You bought this book. You read this book. You thought about what I was saying and wondered if any of it might work for you. Maybe you're trying some things and have even whipped up a little Lo Mein or Chicken Pasta Pesto and your family actually ate it. Maybe you are listening to a little Bob Marley right now. Woohoo! Success everywhere!

Do you know what that means? OK, I want you to take a deep breath and really listen and feel into this.

You are an awesome mom!

Wait, wait. I sense there is a bit of resistance. The drill sergeant is trying to remind you of the time you lost your temper, so let's try it one more time. Deep breath. Close your eyes. Now say it out loud.

I. Am. An. Awesome. Mom.

Alright if you don't love that one, try this:

I am on a journey to becoming the best mom I can be at a given time.

How does that feel? How does your gut react? Does it feel true? If you took the time to read this, think about it, and even try out a few things, then I feel super confident that it's true—deep down in the pit of my stomach true.

And because it's true, let's celebrate you for just a few more minutes together. What does every expert everywhere always say is the most important thing about being a good parent? That you love your child. Goodness gracious, you would have never spent the time reading this book if you didn't love your child. You've already checked the most important box. You care. You love your child. You could just sit back and tell yourself you've already done enough.

But no. You didn't. That wasn't enough for you. You wanted to do more. And because of that you read this book and can now say with complete confidence and truth:

*I am on a journey to becoming the best mom I can be at a given time.*

I hope you can feel how great that feels. If not, just remember every single thing we've talked about, no matter how big or small, is just part of a process. It all takes time. I didn't feel great at the beginning, and I am certainly not done learning and growing. And neither are you. But you are on the path. You are getting better every day. You are a rock star!

And do you know what else I know for sure? You are the perfect person to parent your anxious child. You. There is no one who could do it better than you are doing it. You didn't get the job by default. You are the right person. You got the job and you are going to be great at it.

I know it's a little hard to take all of this in. I've had years and years of practice now listening to my nice voice, and I've had a lot more experience in seeing what my nice voice says is actually true. You haven't had quite as much practice as I've had. This is still a little new to you, and it probably feels a little weird, so I'm just going to ask you to trust me on this one. You are doing great.

Now, does that mean that from here on out life will be sunshine and unicorns, you'll never lose your temper again, and your child's anxious temperament will miraculously never cause them a moment's trouble after today? Of course not. Stuff is going to happen.

But when it does, you've got tools. You've got things to help you stay calm and present. And little by little, your sweetie pie is going to want to try these things that are making a difference in you.

When those tough times come, as they always do for all of us, here are a few things I want you to remember:

- There's no such thing as perfect. You aren't trying to be perfect.
- You are better than you were a year ago. Or last week. You are shooting for progress, not perfection
- Everybody screws up sometimes.
- Every new day is another chance to do better.
- Tiny changes have a huge impact over time.

And one more time because I don't think I can say this enough:

- *You are on a journey*—It's a journey, not a destination.
- *To becoming*—You aren't there; you're still becoming.
- *The best mom you can be*—Just do you. You don't have to be anyone else.
- *At a given time*—All you have is this moment. Do your best with it. And now look! That

moment's already gone. Now do your best with this one.

When the tough times come, use the tools. When you feel like you just can't do it, use the tools. When you want to give up the most, use the tools.

And remember when times seem the absolute worst, this too shall pass. You don't have to get through the next year or the next month. You just have to get through this moment, and you will. You just did.

You rock. I love you. I know you can do it. You are the very best person for your sweetie pie, and she is so, so lucky to have you.

You got this, mama!

# ACKNOWLEDGMENTS

Thank you to Angela Lauria and The Author Incubator's team, as well as to David Hancock and the Morgan James Publishing team for helping me bring this book to print.

This book certainly would not exist without every single one of the amazing clients I've been blessed to know over the years. I wish I could list each of you by name, but you know who you are. To the teenagers, the adults, and everyone in between, I love you. I'm not sure what I did to deserve working with so many truly amazing humans, but you are the best. You inspired me. You challenged me. And I am a better person for having known you.

I am also indebted to the Anxious to Calm in 7 Weeks group. You amazing women brought it week after week. You not only humored me when I said I wanted to create a cross between a podcast and a sleepover, but you jumped in with me. You were honest, supportive, compassionate, and real, and by doing so, we all helped each other feel less isolated and alone. Your presence, your words, and your stories helped heal me and others. Thank you!

To all of my sweet friends who said, "you should write a book" thank you for seeing something that, for a very long time, I didn't see. I have been blessed with the most amazing tribe of friends in various cities all around the world. Shelley, David, Catherine, Carrie, Mark, Michelle, Lynette, Cinnamon, Cindy, Pam, Laura, Linda, LuAnn, Naomi, Paul, Scott, Aimee, John, Ann, PC, Lorrina, Liesel, Emma, Patrick, Craig, Mike, Heleena, Mark, Mindy, Heather, Scott, Catherine, Steve, Kris, Don, Julie, Darrin, Susie, Gerry, Jennifer, Emil, Ilse, Keith, Kathryn, Jay, Danielle, Tara, Morgan, Jessica, and I know I am leaving a few people out but if so, please add your name to this list. You all have been great friends and mean so much to me. I can't imagine being me without the positive influences from every single one of you.

I am grateful to my mother who read stories to me from as early as I can remember and to my dad who gave me his books when I was old enough to read them. And for my PawPaw, the wise and gentle poet who showed me what it meant to love words, and my Meme, Mrs. Collings, the librarian, and voracious reader who was the first enthusiastic reader of my very first "books." And my brother and sister, who still share their books, love, and advice with me.

And last, but certainly not least, my own dear ones. My husband who never fails to encourage all of my crazy ideas, like starting a coaching business and writing a book! My son, Owen, my practice baby, you are a wonderful, kind, smart, and funny young man despite the things I know I've done wrong as your mom. And Amanda, my sweet girl, the blessing I wasn't expecting but have been grateful to receive every day of your life. My wish for you is to be able to see yourself through my eyes so that you can know all of the wonderful, beautiful things you are. You, Crombie family, have been the greatest blessing I have ever received and a testament to God's grace because the wonderful, beautiful, awesomeness of each of you is so much more than I deserve.

## THANK YOU

Thank you so much for reading *Stop Worrying About Your Anxious Child*. Seriously, thank you. I feel like I made a new friend and we just spent the most amazing time laughing and crying and sharing what our lives are like.

Because I am so grateful to you for hanging with me all the way to the end, I've created a short video tutorial where I review everything we've talked about and give a little more guidance. Just pop over to my website (and for you, my new friend, the video is completely free!) It will be like one more chat over coffee.

We've been through a lot together! We can't stop now. I want to hear from you. How's it going? Which parts are easy? What feels hard? You can find me at the links below:

Website: Guidanceforthefuture.com

Email: tonya@guidanceforthefuture.com

Facebook: https://www.facebook.com/guidancefuture

Please keep in touch!

# ABOUT THE AUTHOR

Tonya Crombie is a Martha Beck Institute certified life coach who loves helping parents manage their children's anxiety. She also has a Ph.D. in Industrial and Organizational Psychology and an MBA. Tonya began her career as an organizational and leadership development consultant/executive coach to Fortune 500 companies. After working as a consultant for several years, Tonya accepted an opportunity to work internally within the HR department of a large international hotel company where she progressed to leadership roles in HR and became responsible for employee and organizational development, executive coaching, recruitment and retention, management/leadership development, and succession planning.

In 2003, Tonya left her corporate career behind to focus on ad-hoc project work and one of her first loves, teaching. Tonya authored several courses for distance MBA and Organizational Research degree programs while devoting the majority of her time to being at home with her two young children. In 2012, she founded Guidance for the Future through which she was offered a part-time teaching position where she was able to instruct high school students in areas such as identifying strengths, factors that increase life satisfaction, and using strengths in leadership roles.

She is a requested speaker on the topics of parenting anxious children, leadership, identification and management of strengths, and navigating the way forward when it isn't clear. She lives just outside of New Orleans, Louisiana with her awesome husband, two amazing kids—including a beautifully perfect anxious child—and two extremely barky dogs.

CPSIA information can be obtained
at www.ICGtesting.com
Printed in the USA
JSHW020901200121
11060JS00002BA/69